Simplified PHP

I0016119

James Blanchette PhD

Published by Spangaloo Publishing

Spangaloo Edition

Cover Design: James Bryron Love

Contents

—

Preface

What this book is about, is not to teach you how to program in PHP but to show you more structured way to improve what you're already doing by reusing code and building better functions that will be useful in the long term. Beyond that, working with code that is easily readable and understandable by just applying a few programming practices. This doesn't produce the most efficient code but it does allow you to completely understand what you've written before, to easily make changes at any time.

Probably most importantly providing a different aspect to how you program.

It's time to stop reinventing the wheel every time you have to build a new website. As well to provided list of commands that you are likely to use every day including how to use them and what the parameters mean.

—

What is PHP?

From the preface of the manual:

PHP is an HTML-embedded scripting language. Much of its syntax is borrowed from C, Java and Perl with a couple of unique PHP-specific features thrown in. The goal of the language is to allow web developers to write dynamically generated pages quickly.

What does PHP stand for?

PHP stands for PHP: Hypertext Preprocessor. This confuses many people because the first word of the acronym is the acronym. This type of acronym is called a recursive acronym.

I'd like to start by explaining that PHP is an incredibly complex language, capable of most if not all the things that you would like it to do.

Everything from robust classes to give you object orientated programming, to simply displaying the date on a website. PHP can be utilized using Ajax for dynamic web development that encompasses both server-side and client-side.

Most problems stem from trying to fix code that you wrote six months ago. As you look at it is more difficult to glean any kind of reference to what you are thinking about at the time.

Embedding comments in your files is something that is not only helpful, it is absolutely necessary especially if you need to do some rewrites.

PHP is constantly evolving and as such various commands are either improved and changed or disregarded completely and no longer available.

Simplifying the writing of PHP, to make it easier to understand in the future is what we are going to be talking about. Simplifying the PHP does not make it as efficient as some more complicated versions of the code can be, however readability is what we're after.

Bear in mind that simplifying PHP is not just about writing readable code, it's about being able to reuse the code over and over again thus saving you time, energy and frustration.

—

PHP Basics

This chapter will outline some of the basics of PHP including some of the necessary commands and keywords that you will use it continuously throughout your PHP programming. You can skip this particular chapter if your are you familiar with most of the PHP concepts.

IF ELSE ELSEIF

The if construct or command is available in almost all programming languages. It allows for conditional execution of code. The IF structure itself is similar to that of C programming language.

The expression is evaluated to its boolean value and if the expression is true then the rest of the statement is executed, if it is false that everything gets ignored.

```
if (expr)
statement

if (condition) {
code to be executed if condition is true;
}
```

An example.

```
$t = date("H");
if ($t <= "20") {
echo "Have a good day!";
}else{
echo "Have a good night!";
}
```

By using the else command when the expression is false, we can still do something. It could be to generate an error or output something completely different.
ELSEIF

```
if (condition) {
code to be executed if this condition is true
} elseif (condition) {
code to be executed if this condition is true;
```

—

```
} else {
code to be executed if all conditions are false;
}
```

```
if ( isset ($_SERVER["HTTP_X_FORWARDED"])){
$testip = $_SERVER["HTTP_X_FORWARDED"];
}elseif ( isset ($_SERVER["HTTP_FORWARDED_FOR"])){
$testip = $_SERVER["HTTP_FORWARDED_FOR"];
}elseif ( isset ($_SERVER["HTTP_FORWARDED"])){
$testip = $_SERVER["HTTP_FORWARDED"];
}elseif ( isset ($_SERVER["HTTP_X_FORWARDED"])){
$testip = $_SERVER["HTTP_X_FORWARDED"];
}else{
if ( isset ($_SERVER["REMOTE_ADDR"])){
$testip = $_SERVER["REMOTE_ADDR"];}
}
```

The above code steps through a list of possibilities to grab the user's IP address.

```
$t = date("H");
```

```
if ($t <= "10") {
echo "Have a good morning!";
} elseif ($t <= "20") {
echo "Have a good day!";
} else {
echo "Have a good night!";
}
```

Special characters.

The IF statement generally uses two characters in determining whether a statement is true or not. If it is going to equal something then best practice suggest you use a double Equal sign ==. There are other characters involved and well as can be seen in the above code using the less than <= but also available is the greater than >=. Others are using both greater than and less than two equate to not equal <> as well this != also means not equal to.

There are other ways to express the same thing in a shorter version. Consider this.

```
if ($condition) {
$result = 'foo'
} else {
$result = 'bar'
}
```
can also be expressed this way.

```
$result = $condition ? 'foo' : 'bar';
```

If this $condition evaluates to true, the lefthand operand will be assigned to $result. If the condition evaluates to false, the righthand will be used. As well you can use additional equations as part of a single if statement by using logical operators. You have and, or, XOR,&& || and ! Each performing its own way.

```
if (x==1 and y=2){
}
if (x==1 && y=2){
}
if (x==1 or y=2){
}
```

—

Special conditions also exist , using the triple equal is not the same as using a double equal

```
if($a == $b){
// do something
}
```

Equal true: if $a is equal to $b, after type juggling.

```
if($a === $b){
// do something
}
```

Identical true: if $a is equal to $b, and they are of the same type. So what that means is that if both are integers or perhaps floating-point as well as a string type they can be compared by their type to evaluate whether they're true or not. If you mix an imager with a string and use the triple equal it will always be false.

WHILE

The while command is used in loops and will continue to loop as long as a given condition is true. It also follows a similar structure to the IF command.

while (expr)
statement

The meaning of the while command is simple PHP will execute the necessary men's repeatedly as long as the while at expression evaluates to true. The value is checked at the beginning of the loop so even if the value changes during execution execution will not stop until the end of the iteration.
If the expression evaluates to false then the while command will not execute any code.


```
$x = 1;
while ($x <= 10) {
   echo $x++;
   /* the printed value would be $x before the increment (post-increment) */
   }
```

As well without curly braces.

```
$x = 1;
while ($x <= 10):
   echo $x;
   $x++;
   endwhile;
```

—

Database access heavily utilizes the while command as seen below.

```
$querysub = "select * from sometable order by rand() limit 5";
$resultSub = mysqli_query($con,$querysub) or
die(mysqli_error($con)) ;
if(mysqli_num_rows($resultSub)>=1)
{
//$output[];
while ($getvalue = mysqli_fetch_array($resultSub) )
{
$id=$getvalue["id"];
$value=trim($getvalue["word"]);
// do something with the data
}
}
```

This particular query will loop five times because we've set the limit in the query statement itself to five.

We also use an if command to make sure that we actually have data. The if statement is not fully necessary but his good programming practice to be able to control the unknown.

Our query sub could be different, we can use where statement a like and possibly produce no results from the query, making the if statement more valid to use.

DO WHILE

There is one major difference you should be aware of when using the do--while loop vs. using a simple while loop: And that is when the check condition is made.

In a do--while loop, the test condition evaluation is at the end of the loop. This means that the code inside of the loop will iterate once through before the condition is ever evaluated. This is ideal for tasks that need to execute once before a test is made to continue, such as test that is dependant upon the results of the loop.

Conversely, a plain while loop evaluates the test condition at the beginning of the loop before any execution in the loop block is ever made. If for some reason your test condition evaluates to false at the very start of the loop, none of the code inside your loop will be executed.

```
do {
if ($i < 5) {
echo "i is not big enough";
___ break;
}
$i *= $factor;
if ($i < $minimum_limit) {
break;
}
echo "i is ok";

/* process i */

} while (0);
```

—

FOR NEXT

In most programming languages you have a FOR NEXT
command. In PHP the next is omitted and you simply use the
command FOR.

for (expr1; expr2; expr3)
statement

The first expression (expr1) is evaluated (executed) once
unconditionally at the beginning of the loop.
In the beginning of each iteration, expr2 is evaluated. If it
evaluates to TRUE, the loop continues and the nested
statement(s) are executed. If it evaluates to FALSE, the
execution of the loop ends.
At the end of each iteration, expr3 is evaluated (executed).

/* example 1 */

```
for ($x = 1; $x <= 10; $x++) {
echo $x;
}
```

/* example 3 */

```
$x = 1;
for (; ; ) {
if ($x > 10) {
break;
}
echo $x;
$x++;
}
```

/* example 4 */

```
for ($x = 1, $j = 0; $x <= 10; $j += $x, print $x, $x++);
```

FOR is very useful for single stepping through simple arrays. A simple array consists of a key and a value. Generally the key is a number and that number starts at zero.

```
$fruit = array ("apple", "pear", "peach");
$arrlength = count($fruit);

for ($x = 0; $x < $arrlength; $x++) {
echo $fruit[$x];
echo "<br>";
}
```

As you can see the first argument for FOR is $X equals zero. This represents the start of the array. The second argument is the actual length of the array which we've gotten using the count function. The final argument adds to X by a value of one. That happens at the end of the loop.

Multi dimensional arrays have to be handled differently.

Generally you use the FOR command to loop a given number of times. You can also add other conditional statements that will stop the loop or branch in a different way.

—

FOREACH

FOREACH is most useful in such things as multidimensional arrays.

The foreach construct provides an easy way to iterate over arrays. foreach works only on arrays and objects, and will issue an error when you try to use it on a variable with a different data type or an uninitialized variable. There are two syntaxes:

```
foreach (array_expression as $value)
  statement
foreach (array_expression as $key => $value)
  statement
```

The first example loops over the array given by array expression. On each iteration, the value of the current element is assigned to $value and the internal array pointer is advanced by one (so on the next iteration, you'll be looking at the next element).

The second example will additionally assign the current element's key to the $key variable on each iteration.

```
// first example

$colors = array ("red", "green", "blue", "yellow");

foreach ($colors as $value) {
  echo "$value <br>";
}

// second example
```

```php
$arr = array (1,2,3,4,5,6,7,8,9);

Foreach ($arr as $key => $value)
{
 echo $key;
 echo $value ;
}
```

The above example for the second form is rather simplistic and doesn't really illustrate very well the concept behind a multidimensional array and using FOREACH to actually access that array.

```php
// Multidimensional array

$superheroes = array(
batman" => array(
"name" => "Bruce Wayne",
"email" => "batman@batcave.com",
),

 "super-man" => array(
"name" => "Clark Kent",
"email" => "clarkkent@dailyplanet.com",
),

 "iron-man" => array(
"name" => "Tony Stark",
"email" => "ironman@stark.com",
)
);

// Printing all the keys and values one by one

$keys = array_keys ($superheroes);

for($i = 0; $i < count ($superheroes); $i++) {
```

—

```php
echo $keys[$i] . "{<br>";

foreach ($superheroes [$keys[$i]] as $key => $value) {
echo $key . " : " . $value . "<br>";

}

echo "}<br>";

}
```

From the code the array starts with a number, also has a key name. So take in the case of the third array piece, it is called ironman. Further it has two elements and not just one. In this case the name and the email.

We have to use two different types of loops to access the data. The first is a FOR and the second is a FOREACH. This will output first the name of the key and then second the secondary keys and their value. More on arrays to be covered later, including json arrays.

SWITCH

The switch command bears similarities to the IF command comparing the same expression. You may want to compare the same variable or expression with different values and then branch the code depending on what the value equals to. It also can contain a default value when everything else is false.

The first example shows how this is done using IF and ELSEIF.

```
if ($x == 0) {
 echo "i equals 0";
} elseif ($x == 1) {
 echo "i equals 1";
} elseif ($x == 2) {
 echo "i equals 2";
}
```

The second example shows the switch command.

```
switch ($x) {
case 0:
 echo "x equals 0";
 break;
case 1:
 echo "x equals 1";
 break;
case 2:
 echo "x equals 2";
 break;
default:
 echo " Nothing matches";
 break;
}
```

—

With the switch command there's also another command that is useful, called break. Once the expression has been found and is true it discontinues further processing and exits the switch.

The next example gives the basic layout of the switch command. Most notable is that case can be a variable that is a number, string or an expression.

```
switch (n) {
case label1:
code to be executed if n=label1;
break;
case label2:
code to be executed if n=label2;
break;
case label3:
code to be executed if n=label3;
break;
default:
code to be executed if n is different from all labels;
}

$mycolor = "red";

switch ($mycolor) {
case "red":
echo "I like the color red!";
break;
case "blue":
echo "I like the color blue!";
break;
case "green":
echo "I like the color green!";
break;
default:
```

```
        echo "My Color is neither red, blue, nor green!";
    }
```

Please note that when you are using a string in the switch statement as an expression to evaluate for, it is case sensitive so when it is checking the $mycolour variable Red is not the same as red.

As well the case whether you checking for an integer or string etc. uses: and not a semicolon.

—

TRIM

trim — Strip whitespace (or other characters) from the beginning and end of a string

ltrim() - Removes whitespace or other predefined characters from the left side of a string
rtrim() - Removes whitespace or other predefined characters from the right side of a string

This function returns a string with whitespace stripped from the beginning and end of str. Without the second parameter, trim() will strip these characters:

" " (ASCII 32 (0x20)), an ordinary space.
"\t" (ASCII 9 (0x09)), a tab.
"\n" (ASCII 10 (0x0A)), a new line (line feed).
"\r" (ASCII 13 (0x0D)), a carriage return.
"\0" (ASCII 0 (0x00)), the NUL-byte.
"\x0B" (ASCII 11 (0x0B)), a vertical tab.

```
function trim_array(&$value)
{
$value = trim($value);
}

$fruit = array('apple','pear ',' cherry ');
var_dump($fruit);


array(3) {
[0]=>
string(5) "apple"
[1]=>
```

```
string(5) "pear "
[2]=>
string(8) " cherry "
}

array_walk($fruit, 'trim_array');
var_dump($fruit);

array(3) {
  [0]=>
  string(5) "apple"
  [1]=>
  string(4) "pear"
  [2]=>
  string(6) "cherry"
}
```

When specifying the character mask you use double quotes as single quotes will not work correctly.

```
$hello = "
  Hello World "; //here is a string with some trailing and
leading whitespace

$trimmed_correct = trim($hello, " \t\n\r"); //<--------
OKAY
$trimmed_incorrect = trim($hello, ' \t\n\r'); //<--------NOT
AS EXPECTED

print ("----------------------------");
print ("TRIMMED OK:"."<br>");
print_r($trimmed_correct."<br>");
print ("----------------------------");
print ("TRIMMING NOT OK:"."<br>");
print_r($trimmed_incorrect."<br>");
```

—

```
print ("---------------------------"."<br>");
```

Here is the output:

```
---------------------------TRIMMED OK:
Hello World
---------------------------TRIMMING does not work:

 Hello World
---------------------------
```

Remove characters from both sides of a string ("He" in "Hello" and "d!" in "World"):

```
$str = "Hello World!";
echo $str . "<br>";
echo trim($str,"Hed!");
```

Will out put something like this
With out trim
Hello World!

With trim
llo Worl

The same rules apply to LTRIM and RTRIM.

STRINGS

A string is series of characters, each character is the same as a byte. PHP only supports a 256-character set, and does not offer native Unicode support.

Note: As of PHP 7.0.0, there are no real restrictions regarding the length of a string on 64-bit builds. On 32-bit builds and in earlier versions, a string is limited up to 2GB (2147483647 bytes)

Details of the String Type ¶

The string in PHP is implemented as an array of bytes and an integer indicating the number of characters in the buffer.
It has no information about how those bytes translate to characters, leaving that task to the programmer.
There are no limitations on the values the string can be composed of; in particular, bytes with value 0 ("NUL bytes") are allowed anywhere in the string
(however, a in few functions, may not to be "binary safe", may hand off the strings to libraries that ignore alldata after a NUL byte.)

This nature of the string type explains why there is no separate "byte" type in PHP – strings take this role.
Functions that return no textual data ie. arbitrary data read from a network socket, will still return it as a string or a series of strings.

—

Most important to note is that PHP does not natively handle Unicode however it can still be work with and using multibyte strings and correctly setting encodings will work. Perhaps the biggest challenge is making sure that it works all the time in every function that you are using. This requires a lot of testing on the programmer side to ensure that every thing works as expected.

See the appendix for a full list of all commands (functions) that deal with strings.

STR_REPLACE

str_replace (find,replace,string,count)

The str_replace () command replaces some characters with some other characters in a string or array.
STR_REPLACE is case senstive.

This function works by the following rules:
If the string to be searched is string, it returns a string. __
If the string to be searched is an array, it returns an array.
If the string to be searched is an array, find and replace is performed with every array element.
If both find and replace are arrays, and replace has fewer elements than find, an empty string will be used as replace.
If find is an array and replace is a string, the replace string will be used for every find value.

Note: This function is case-sensitive. Use the str_ireplace() command to perform a case-insensitive search.

Note: This function is binary-safe.

Parameter __ Description
find __ Required. Specifies the value to find
replace __ Required. Specifies the value to replace the value in find
string __ Required. Specifies the string to be searched
count __ Optional. A variable that counts the number of replacements

$string = "It was nice meeting you."
str_replace ('you', 'him', $string)

—

Output: It was nice meeting him.

$str = "You eat fruits, vegetables, fiber every day."
$array1 = array("fruits", "vegetables", "fiber")
$array2 = array("nachos", "wine", "beans")
str_replace ($array1, $array2, $str)
Output: You eat nachos, wine, beans every day.

str_ireplace() is the same as str_replace except that it is case insensitive. IE Dog dog is the same where as in str_replace () if you are replacing dog , it will not replace Dog.

This command, str_replace (), is very powerful and is best use for controlling input as well as output. When used a security measure, is capable of stripping input that a hacker may use to attempt to gain access to your database or bad user input.
Generally we are looking at stripping input that comes from a user in the form of a text box on a form and/or textarea. The input can also come from a database.

$input$_Post['textarea1'];

$output=trim($input);
$output=str_replace ("."," ",$output); // replace . with '
$output=str_replace (" | ","",$output); // get rid of More Pipe
$output=str_replace ('$',"",$output); // get rid of dollar signs
$output=str_replace ('"',"",$output); // get rid of double quotes
$output=str_replace ("'","",$output); // get rid of single quotes
$output=str_replace ('{',"",$output); // get rid of braces
$output=str_replace ('}',"",$output); // get rid of braces
$output=str_replace ('[',"",$output); // get rid of brackets
$output=str_replace (']',"",$output); // get rid of brackets

This illustrates technique for manually stripping the input. There are other commands that can be used *as well including preg_replace*

```
$result = preg_replace ('/abc/', 'def', $string); # Replace all 'abc' with 'def'
$result = preg_replace ('/abc/i', 'def', $string); # Replace with case insensitive matching
$result = preg_replace ('/\s+/', '', $string); # Strip all whitespaces
$result = preg_replace ('/abc(def)hij/', '/\ \1/', $string);

# Strip HTML tag
$result = preg_replace ('#<span id="15">.*</span>#m', '', $string);
```

The command preg_replace can be extremely complex using various regex and will be covered later.

```
$string = '漢字はユニコード';
$needle = 'は';
$replace = 'Foo';

echo str_replace ($needle, $replace, $string);
// outputs: 漢字Fooユニコード
```

NOTE:
The usual problem is that the string is evaluated as binary string, meaning PHP is not aware of encodings at all.

Problems arise if you are getting a value "from outside sources" (database, POST request) and the encoding of the needle and the haystack is not the same type.

That usually means the source code is not saved in the same encoding as you are receiving "from outside sources". Therefore the binary representations don't match and nothing happens. There are ways to change the encoding types to match.

—

EXPLODE

The explode command is very handy for breaking apart strings for the given parameter. If so you have text input from a text area and its several paragraphs long but you need to do a spelling test on each word, the easiest way is to explode it into an array and then test each word.

The explode() function breaks a string into an array.
Note: The "separator" parameter cannot be an empty string.
Note: This function is binary-safe.

Explode (*separator, string, limit*)

Parameter __ Description
separator __ Required. Specifies where to break the string
string __ Required. The string to split
limit __ Optional. Specifies the number of array elements to return.

Possible values:

- Greater than 0 - Returns an array with a maximum of *limit* element(s)
- Less than 0 - Returns an array except for the last -*limit* elements()
- 0 - Returns an array with one element

- If limit not set return all elements

<u>An example.</u>

function checkWord ($word){
  global $con;

—

```php
$querysub = "select * from speller where tword ='$word' limit
1";
    $resultSub = mysqli_query ($con, $querysub) or
die(mysqli_error ($con)) ;
        If (mysqli_num_rows ($resultSub)>=1)
        {
        // found word
        return 1;
        }else{
        // word not found
        return 0;
        }
}
//make connection to the database
global $con; // must be set to global to use in functions and set
before it is used

$con = new mysqli($it_db_host, $it_db_user,
$it_db_pwd,$it_db_name); //connect to MySql
    if ($con->connect_error) {//Output any connection error
    die('Error : ('. $con->connect_errno .') '. $con->connect_error);
    }
$message =$_POST ['theparagraph'];
$estring = explode (" ",$newstring);
foreach ($estring as $word){
    $word=trim ($word);
    //remove all puncution that can interfer with finding the correct
word
    $newstring =str_replace ("\r\n", "",$word); // remove newline
and carriage returns
    $newstring =str_replace ("\n", "",$newstring);// remove
newline
    $newstring =str_replace (" ", "",$newstring);/ convert all
spaces to nothing
    $newstring =str_replace (",", " ",$newstring);
    $newstring =str_replace ('"', " ",$newstring);
    $newstring =str_replace ("'", " ",$newstring);
```

```
$newstring =str_replace ('"', " ",$newstring);
$newstring =str_replace ('"', " ",$newstring);
$newstring =str_replace ('.', " . ",$newstring);
$newstring =str_replace ('?', " ? ",$newstring);
$newstring =str_replace ('!', " ! ",$newstring);
$newstring =str_replace (';', " ; ",$newstring);

$word=$newstring;

$tword=strtolower ($word);// make word lowercase
// test the word against existing data from database or large
array using the function we made called check spelling
$ck=checkSpelling($word);
  if ($ck==1){
  //
  //word spelled correctly;

  }else{
  //echo "Spelling ERROR $word <br>";

  }
}
```

In the above example, we're getting data from the user in the form of the text area(not shown) however this data could come from a text file, a document that was uploaded and then converted to text were a variety of other methods.

We use the explode command to break apart the paragraph into single words as well as stripping all punctuation out and removing unnecessary spaces. Once we've accomplished that we can now check the spelling of the word against our database. You can also use a large array to check the spelling of each word.

—

The parameter for exploding can be set to anything you want, in this case we are exploding using spaces but you can use a comma or any other delimiter.

```
$estring =explode (",",$newstring);
$estring =explode (" | ",$newstring);
$estring =explode e("#",$newstring);
$estring =explode (" |-| ",$newstring);
```

String Change case

strtolower() strtoupper() ucfirst() ucwords().
All the above same syntax but he says something slightly different.

strtolower() converts the entire string to lowercase.
strtoupper() converts the entire string to uppercase
ucfirst() converts the first character in the first word in the string to uppercase.
ucwords()converts the first character of each word in a string to uppercase.

Syntax.
strtolower (*string*)
Note: This function is binary-safe.

echo strtolower ("My what a Wonderful WORLD.");

will output

my what a wonderful world.

$str="My what a Wonderful WORLD."
echo strtolower ($str);

will also output

my what a wonderful world.

You may also notice that because we using the string $str, we are not using any form of quotes inside the parentheses. Single quotes and double quotes are only used for literals which are generally hand coded at that point.

—

Syntax.
strtoupper (*string*)

echo strtoupper *("My what a Wonderful WORLD.");*

will output

MY WHAT A WONDERFUL WORLD.

Syntax.
ucfirst (*string*)

echo ucfirst *("my what a Wonderful WORLD.");*

will output
My what a Wonderful WORLD

Syntax.
ucwords (*string*)

echo ucwords *("my what a Wonderful WORLD.");*

will output
My What A Wonderful WORLD.

SUBSTR

substr is useful for just returning parts of a string and can be utilized in a variety of different ways. The below examples will only examine the simplest ways to use it, however using a series of commands the substr command can be used for complicated text files that need to be converted to say a database or used in other ways. The last example will detail how using several string commands at a time we can accomplish something wonderful.

string substr (string $string , int $start [, int $length])
Returns the portion of string specified by the start and length parameters.

substr (*string,start,length*)

Parameter __ Description
string __ Required. Specifies the string to return a part of
start __ Required. Specifies where to start in the string
 • A positive number - Start at a specified position in the string
 • A negative number - Start at a specified position from the end of the string

 • 0 - Start at the first character in string
length __ Optional. Specifies the length of the returned string. Default is to the end of the string.
 • A positive number - The length to be returned from the start parameter

 • Negative number - The length to be returned from the end of the string

—

Version __ Description

7.0.0 __ If string is equal to start characters long, an empty string will be returned. Prior to this version, FALSE was returned in this case.

5.2.2 - 5.2.6 __ If the start parameter indicates the position of a negative truncation or beyond, false is returned. Other versions get the string from start.

```
// Positive numbers:
echo substr ("Hello world",0,10)."<br>";
outputs Hello worl
echo substr ("Hello world",1,8)."<br>";
outputs ello wor
echo substr ("Hello world",0,5)."<br>";
outputs Hello
echo substr ("Hello world",6,6)."<br>";
outputs world

// Negative numbers:
echo substr ("Hello world",0,-1)."<br>";
outputs Hello worl
echo substr ("Hello world",-10,-2)."<br>";
outputs ello wor
echo substr ("Hello world",0,-6)."<br>";
outputs Hello
```

Please note the subtle differences in PHP 7 and how it modifies the output when using sub string functions. Instead of returning a false value, it returns an empty string. See the following example for clarity.

```
class apple {
    public function __ toString() {
    return "green";
}
```

```
}
```

echo "1) ".var_expor t(substr ("pear", 0, 2), true).PHP_EOL;
echo "2) ".var_export (substr (54321, 0, 2), true).PHP_EOL;
echo "3) ".var_export (substr (new apple(), 0, 2), true).PHP_EOL;
echo "4) ".var_export (substr (true, 0, 1), true).PHP_EOL;
echo "5) ".var_export (substr (false, 0, 1), true).PHP_EOL;
echo "6) ".var_export (substr ("", 0, 1), true).PHP_EOL;
echo "7) ".var_export (substr (1.2e3, 0, 4), true).PHP_EOL;

Output of the above example in PHP 7:

```
1) 'pe'
2) '54'
3) 'gr'
4) '1'
5) ''
6) ''
7) '1200'
```

Output of the above example in PHP 5:

```
1) 'pe'
2) '54'
3) 'gr'
4) '1'
5) false
6) false
7) '1200'
```

A real world example

$file = "KEY: Conjecture , - n,[See SUPPOSE].KEY: Conjecture ,
- v.
SYN: guest,divination,hypothesis,theory,notion,surmise,
supposition.
ANT: Computation,calculation,inference,reckoning,proof,
deduction.
KEY: Conquest,[See CONQUER].
SYN: Victory,triumph,overthrow,discomfiture,subjugation.

—

```
ANT: Failure,defeat,retreat,surrender,forfeiture,submission,
discomfiture.";
$file = str_replace("\n"," ", $file);
$stringlength = strlen($file);
$scounter = $stringlength - 1;
echo " looking for KEY <br>";
//$pos=strpos($file,'KEY:',strpos($file,'KEY:') + 1);


//echo "POS =$pos <br>";


//echo get_string_between($file, "KEY:", "KEY:");
//substr (string, start, length)
//$test = substr ($file, 0, $pos);
//echo $test ."<hr>";
//do until $second> = $stringlength{
$firstp = 0;
$secondp = 1;
echo "secondp $secondp scounter $scounter <br>";
$x = 0;
//while($secondp < =$scounter){
while($secondp < =$scounter){


echo "secondp $secondp scounter $scounter <br>";
//$firstp = $pos;
//$pos=strpos($file,'KEY:',strpos($file,'KEY:') + $fpos);
//$first=strpos($file,"KEY:",$fpos + 1 );
echo "First $firstp <br>";


$secondp = strpos($file,"KEY:",$firstp + 4 );
if ($secondp == 0){
$secondp =$stringlength;
}
//$secondp = strpos_offset_recursive("KEY:", $file, 2);
//$secondp = strpos($file,"KEY:",$firstp + 1);
echo "Second $secondp <br>";


//echo "POS = $pos <br>";
```

```php
$test2 = substr ($file, $firstp, $secondp - $firstp);
// now we break apart what we got= > ,
// KEYKEY: Conquest,[See CONQUER].
$testlen = strlen($test2);
echo " Length $testlen <br>";
$tsyn = strpos($test2,"SYN:" ) ; //$firstp + 4 )
if ($tsyn == 0){
$syn = "";
$key = trim(substr ($test2, 4, $testlen));
$ant = "";
$kete = strpos($key,"," ) ;
if ($kete> = 1){
echo "found KETE - 1 $kete TSYN $tsyn<br>";
$key = trim(substr ($key, 0, $kete ));
// substr (string, start, length)
$keylen = strlen($key);
echo "KEYLEN $keylen <br>";
$keyextra =trim(substr ($test2, $kete +6, ($testlen - $keylen)));
}else{
$keyextra = "";
}
}else{
$key = trim(substr ($test2, 4, $tsyn- 4));
$kete = strpos($key,"," ) ;
if ($kete> = 1){
echo "found KETE - 2 $kete <br>";
$keylen = strlen($key);
echo "KEYLEN $keylen <br>";

$keyextra =trim(substr ($key, $kete +1, ($keylen)));
$key = trim(substr ($key, 0, $kete ));
}else{
$keyextra = "";
}
$tant = strpos($test2,"ANT:" );
if ($tant == 0){
$tant = $testlen;
```

—

```
}
$syn =substr ($test2, $tsyn+4, $tant - ($tsyn+4));

if ($tant == 0){
$ant = "";
}else{
$ant = substr ($test2, $tant+4, $testlen);
}
}
// figure out what is in the string
$tkey = $key;
echo " KEY $tkey <br>";
echo " SYN $syn <br>";
echo " ANT $ant <br>";
echo " Extra $keyextra <br>";
echo "<hr>";
$firstp = $secondp;
}
```

STRPOS

(PHP 4, PHP 5, PHP 7)
strpos - Find the position of the first occurrence of a substring in a string.
PHP 7.1.0 __ Support for negative offsets has been added.

int strpos (string $haystack , mixed $needle [, int $offset = 0])
Returns an integer value.

haystack

The string to search in.
needle

If needle is not a string, it is converted to an integer and applied as the ordinal value of a character.
offset (Optional)
If specified, search will start this number of characters counted from the beginning of the string. If the offset is negative, the search will start this number of characters counted from the end of the string.

Returns the position of where the needle exists relative to the beginning of the haystack string (independent of offset). Also note that string positions start at 0, and not 1.

Returns FALSE if the needle was not found.
Warning
This function may return Boolean FALSE, but may also return a non-Boolean value which evaluates to FALSE (ZERO). Use the === (triple operator) for testing the return value of this command.

—

```php
$string = 'abcdefghi';
$needle = 'a';
$pos = strpos($string, $needle);

// Note our use of ===.Simply == would not work as
expected
// because the position of 'a' was the 0th (first) character.
using === ( triple operator )
if ($pos === false) {
echo "The string $needle was not found in the string
$string";
 } else {
echo "The string $needle was found in$string";
echo " and exists at position $pos";
}

OR using !== ( triple operator )
if ($pos !== false) {
echo "The string $needle was found in $string";
 echo " and exists at position $pos";
} else {
echo "The string $needle was not found in$string";
}

Using an offset

$newstring = 'abcdef abcdef';
$pos = strpos($newstring, 'a', 1); // $pos = 7, not 0
```

Related functions:

strrpos() - Finds the position of the last occurrence of a string inside another string (case-sensitive)
stripos() - Finds the position of the first occurrence of a string inside another string (case-insensitive)

strripos() - Finds the position of the last occurrence of a string inside another string (case-insensitive)

—

STRLEN

(PHP 4, PHP 5, PHP 7)

strlen — Get string length

int strlen (string $string)

Returns the length of the given string as an integer.
The length of the string on success, and 0 if the string is empty.

echo strlen ("Hello");
Outputs 5

Note:

strlen() returns the number of bytes rather than the number of characters in a string.
strlen() returns NULL when executed on arrays, and an E_WARNING level error is emitted.
On arrays use COUNT
If you want to get the number of characters in a string of UTF8 so use mb_strlen() instead of strlen().
However
Another way to get character count of a UTF8 string is to pass the text through utf8_decode() first:

$length = strlen(utf8_decode ($somestring));

utf8_decode() converts characters that are not in ISO-8859-1 to '?', which, for the purpose of counting works.

STRSTR

strstr(string,search,before_search)
The strstr() command searches for the first occurrence of a string inside another string.

Note:
This function is binary-safe.
This function is case-sensitive. For a case-insensitive search, use stristr() function.

Parameter __ Description
string __ Required. Specifies the string to search
search __ Required. Specifies the string to search for. If this parameter is a number, it will search for the character matching the ASCII value of the number
before_search __ Optional. A boolean value whose default is "false". If set to "true", it returns the part of the string before the first occurrence of the *search* parameter.

```
$email= 'franticbob@somedomain.com';
$domain = strstr ($email, '@');
echo $domain; // outputs @somedomain.com

$user = strstr ($email, '@', true); // As of PHP 5.3.0
echo $user; // outputs franticbob
```

—

ARRAYS

An array is a data structure that stores one or more similar type of data values in a single varible.

For example if you want to store 50 pieces of data instead of defining multiple variables , one for each, they can be stored in one variable.

You then use loops to retrieve it.

There are three different kind of arrays and each array value is accessed using an IDwhich is called array index.

Numeric array – An array with a numeric index. Values are stored and accessed in linear fashion by the number.All Numeric arrays Start at 0 (zero) and not 1.

Associative array – An array with strings as index. This stores element values in association with key values rather than in a strict numbered index order.

Multidimensional array – An array containing one or more arrays and values are accessed using multiple indices

An array can be created using the array() language construct. It takes any number of comma-separated key => value pairs as arguments.

```
array(
key => value,
key2 => value2,
key3 => value3,
)
```

As of PHP 5.4 you can also use the short array syntax, which replaces *array()* with *[]*.

```
$array = array(
"food" => "bread",
"drink" => "beer",
```

```
);

// as of PHP 5.4
$array = [
"food" => "bread",
"drink" => "beer",
];
```

Numeric Arrays
Are considered to be single dimension arrays.
$myarray = array("Brina", "Harold", "Fred", "Tim");

These are rather easy to build and can be made from data acquired many different sources as well as database.
The can also be written completely different way.

```
$myarray = array(
"Brina",
"Harold",
"Fred",
"Tim"
);
```

In this array the index consists of numbers and in this case it will be numbers 0 to 3 because it has four elements.
Accessing the array is quite easy because we simply loop through it using a FOR loop.

```
$length = count($myarray);
for($x = 0; $x < $length; $x++) {
echo $myarray[$x];
echo "<br>";
}
```
Or you could use this.

```
echo "I like " . $myarray [0] . ", " . $myarray [1] . " and " . $myarray [2] . " but not ". $myarray [3].".";
```

—

ISSET

ISSET is an extremely useful command that can save you hours of time looking for errors in your code. Tracking down errors from unset variables is not necessarily straightforward because the line number for the error may not correspond to the actual problem. Checking to see if a variable is there before it is used is particularly useful in arrays. Before you use FOR or FOREACH to step through an array it is handy to know if the array is actually available. If the array does not exist, you will encounter a parse error in tracking down the problem may be difficult. The command is fairly easy to use and it takes a single or multiple variables and basically tells you if they are set.

From a programming viewpoint the philosophy is checked before you use it.

(PHP 4, PHP 5, PHP 7)
isset — Determine if a variable is set and is not NULL

Parameter:

Name __ Description __ Required/ Optional __ Type

Variable1 __ The variable being checked __ Required __ Mixed*

Variable2 ...... __ More variable to be checked. __ Optional __ Mixed*

*Mixed: Mixed indicates that a parameter may accept multiple (but not necessarily all) types.

NOTE:

isset() only works with variables as passing anything else will result in a parse error. For checking if constants are set use the defined() function.

Return value:
TRUE if variable (variable1,variable2..) exists and has value not equal to NULL, FALSE otherwise.
Value Type: Boolean.

```php
$var = '';

// This will evaluate to TRUE so the text will be printed
// even though $var doesn't contain any characters etc but
// because it has been set.
if (isset($var)) {
echo "This var is set so it can be used.";
}

// In the next examples we'll use var_dump to output
// the return value of isset().

$a = "test1";
$b = "anothertest";

var_dump (isset($a));// TRUE
var_dump (isset($a, $b)); // TRUE

unset ($a);

var_dump (isset($a)); // FALSE
var_dump (isset($a, $b)); // FALSE

$foo = NULL;
var_dump(isset($foo)); // FALSE
```

—

This also work for elements in arrays:

```
$a = array ('test' => 1, 'hello' => NULL, 'pie' => array('a' =>
'apple'));

var_dump (isset($a['test']));// TRUE
var_dump (isset($a['jungle'])); // FALSE
var_dump (isset($a['hello'])); // FALSE

// The key 'hello' equals NULL so is considered unset
// If you want to check for NULL key values then try:
var_dump (array_key_exists('hello', $a)); // TRUE

// Checking deeper array values
var_dump (isset($a['pie']['a']));// TRUE
var_dump (isset($a['pie']['b']));// FALSE
var_dump (isset($a['cake']['a']['b']));// FALSE
```

All the above examples illustrate the values returned.

Often times you want to do a particular section of code based upon whether or not a variable is set. Forms that the user has filled out need to be processed and there's a variety ways to do this.

```
<!DOCTYPE html PUBLIC "-//W3C//DTD XHTML 1.0
Transitional//EN" "http://www.w3.org/TR/xhtml1/DTD/xhtml1-
transitional.dtd">
<html xmlns="http://www.w3.org/1999/xhtml">
<head>
<meta content="text/html; charset=utf-8" http-equiv="Content-
Type" />
<title>FormTest</title>
</head>

<body>
<?
```

```php
if (isset ($_POST ['Hidden1'])){
// Hidden1 is set so we process the form
    if (isset ($_POST ['Text1'])){
    // we do some stuff
    }

}else{
// continue on with the script
?>

<form action="somepage.php" method="post">
<br />
<input name = "Text1" type="text" /><br />
<input name = "Hidden1" type="hidden" value = "1" /><br />
<br />
<input name = "Submit1" type="submit" value="submit" /><br
/>
</form>
<?
}
?>
</body>
</html>
```

In the example above, the first time the page loads, the Post variable Hidden1 has not been set so the form is displayed. Once the user enters information and clicks on the submit button the variable POST['Hidden1'] is now set and will be processed once the page loads again.

—

COUNT

(PHP 4, PHP 5, PHP 7)

count — Count all elements in an array, or something in an object

Return the number of elements in an array:

count(ARRAY,MODE);
$arraycount=count($myarray,0);

Syntax

Parameter __ Description
ARRAY __ Required. Specifies the array
MODE __ Optional. Specifies the mode. Possible values:

- 0 - Default. Does not count all elements of multidimensional arrays

- 1 - Counts the array recursively (counts all the elements of multidimensional arrays)

*$foods = array ('fruits' => array('pear', 'plum', 'peach'),
'vegetable' => array ('celery', 'spinach', 'tomato'));*

// recursive count
echo count ($foods, COUNT_RECURSIVE); // output 8
echo count ($foods, 1); // output 8

// normal count
echo count ($foods); // output 2
echo count ($foods,0); // output 2

These will produce a warning error as of php 7.2

```php
<?
echo "Test counting NULL <br>";
echo count(null); // outputs 0
echo "<br>Test counting False <br>";

echo count(false); // output 1
?>
```

Warning: count(): Parameter must be an array or an object that implements Countable in on line 3 // as of PHP 7.2
   int(0)

Warning: count(): Parameter must be an array or an object that implements Countable in on line 6 // as of PHP 7.2
   int(1)

Note:
Because this is a language construct and not a function, it cannot be called using <u>variable functions</u>.
   (*see the PHP manual for a description of variable functions.*)
When using empty() on inaccessible object properties, the __ isset() overloading method will be called, if declared.

—

TIME

Being able to get and set various aspects of time is essential to a lot of PHP programming. The command time() produces a timestamp in seconds. There are also other ways to utilize time and that is using the date command. In the date command, if the timestamp is left out then now is assumed. As well all timestamps, dates etc. are assumed from the actual server time. You can set a local time zone rather easily as well. A complete list of time zones is available in the appendix.

NOTE:

the UNIX timestamp is a signed 32-bit binary integer and subject to the limitations of that. Essentially that means in the year 2038 the timestamp runs out of digits available and reverts back to a negative number effectively representing 13 December 1901.

The latest time that can be represented in Unix's signed 32-bit integer time format is 03:14:07 UTC on Tuesday, 19 January 2038 (2,147,483,647 seconds after 1 January 1970)

Programs that work with future dates will begin to run into problems sooner; for example a program that works with dates 20 years in the future should have been fixed no later than 19 January 2018. There is currently not a workaround for this even though now most UNIX and Linux systems internally use a 64-bit time value to calculate dates. There are many programs that need to be changed and/or fixed including various database software like MYSql, Oracle, MariaDB as well as others because they rely on various aspects of 32-bit timestamps as part of their structure for data.

You have to be particularly careful with working with dates especially if those dates extend into the future but doing long calculations in numbers for mortgage calculations or any other code that has to work over the course of many years. Consequently a 64 bit signed integer as a timeout value of 292 billion years so we won't have to worry about that for a while once it's been implemented.

(PHP 4, PHP 5, PHP 7)

time — Return current Unix timestamp
Description ¶
int time (void)

Returns the current time measured in the number of seconds since the Unix Epoch (January 1 1970 00:00:00 GMT) based on the current server time or time zone setting if set differently from the server.

```php
<?php
$nextWeek = time() + (7 * 24 * 60 * 60);
// 7 days; 24 hours; 60 mins; 60 secs
echo 'Now: '. date('Y-m-d') ."<br>";
echo 'Next Week: '. date('Y-m-d', $nextWeek) ."<br>";
// or using strtotime():
echo " Using strtotime <br>";
echo 'Next Week: '. date('Y-m-d', strtotime('+1 week')) ."<br>";
?>
```
Outputs

Now: 2018-09-15
Next Week: 2018-09-22
Using strtotime
Next Week: 2018-09-22

—

date

(PHP 4, PHP 5, PHP 7)

date — Format a local time/date
Description ¶
string date (string $format [, int $timestamp = time()])

Returns a string formatted according to the given format string using the given integer timestamp or the current time if no timestamp is given. In other words, timestamp is optional and defaults to the value of time().

$timestring = time();

Full Date

$humandate = date("F j, Y, g:i a", $timestring);
*echo $humandate."
";*
September 16, 2018, 3:13 am

Full Date Short
$humandate = date("F j, Y", $timestring);
*echo $humandate."
";*
September 16, 2018

Using it in a form to select dates

This utilizes a function to populate a form for selecting month and year.

function DateSelector($inName, $useDate=0)
{
/ create array so we can name months */*

```php
$monthName = array(1 => "January", "February", "March",
"April", "May", "June", "July", "August",
"September", "October", "November", "December");

/* if date invalid or not supplied, use current time */
if ($useDate == 0)
{
$useDate = Time();
}

/* make month selector */
echo "<SELECT NAME=" . $inName . "Month>\n";
for ($currentMonth = 1; $currentMonth<= 12;
$currentMonth++)
{
echo "<OPTION VALUE=\"";
echo intval ($currentMonth);
echo "\"";
if (intval (date( "m", $useDate)) == $currentMonth)
{
echo " SELECTED";
}
echo ">" . $monthName [$currentMonth] . "\n";
}
echo "</SELECT>";

/* make day selector */
echo "<SELECT NAME=" . $inName . "Day>\n";
for ($currentDay=1; $currentDay<= 31; $currentDay++)
{
echo "<OPTION VALUE=\"$currentDay\"";
if (intval (date( "d", $useDate)) == $currentDay)
{
echo " SELECTED";
}
echo ">$currentDay\n";
}
```

—

```php
echo "</SELECT>";

/* make year selector */
echo "<SELECT NAME=" . $inName . "Year>\n";
$startYear = date( "Y", $useDate);
for ($currentYear = $startYear - 5; $currentYear<=
$startYear+5; $currentYear++)
{
echo "<OPTION VALUE=\"$currentYear\"";
if (date ( "Y", $useDate) == $currentYear)
{
echo " SELECTED";
}
echo ">$currentYear\n";
}
echo "</SELECT>";

}
```

Sessions

(PHP 4 >= 4.1.0, PHP 5, PHP 7)
$_SESSION -- $HTTP_SESSION_VARS [deprecated] —
Session variables.

Is an associative array containing session variables available
to the current script.

Note:

This is a **superglobal**, or automatic global, variable. This means
that it is available in all scopes throughout a script without theneed
to do **global $variable;** to access it within functions or methods.

Each can be accessed through its command, see the
appendix section for a full list of available functions for
sessions.

A session is a way to store information (in variables) to be
used across multiple pages.

Unlike a cookie, the information is stored on the server and
not the users computer.

If you open up an application on your computer and do
some changes and close it, this is similar to a session. Your
computer knows you all and about the application like when
it starts and stops but on the Internet, the HTTP address does
not maintain a state.

Session variables solve this problem by storing user
information that is accessible across multiple pages on a
website. Session variables can be set that can hold such things
as usernames and other useful information.

—

All of this becomes unique to the individual in a separate session is open for each visitor on the website.

Before sessions can be used, they have to be initialized and this should be at the very start of your PHP page.

session_start --- Start new or resume existing session

```
<?
session_start();
```

Please notice that this is the first line script after the PHP tag <? .

If you do not start a session, you cannot use any session variables and session commands may not return any data. That is why it is common practice to insert session_start() into every webpage that will be using sessions and even those that aren't because the user may go back to a page it does use them.

After you started the session you can then access the functions or commands that are available.

One of interest is session_id. This is an unique identification that is put together from a lot of different information.

c3547196279001ced81f0a94d2017fb6 is an example of the session ID.

```
session_start();
$xx = session_id();
echo $xx;
```

output
c3547196279001ced81f0a94d2017fb6

There are other ways to make uses of sessions and one is to create your own session variables.

```
$_SESSION ["username"] = $username;
$_SESSION ["login"] = 1;
$_SESSION ["username"] = "someuser";
$_SESSION ["login"] = 0;
```

Session variables are stored in an array format that uses key and value.

When you're switching pages, retaining the necessary information like whether or not a user is logged in or not is vital.

Accessing the information only requires you to use the key to get the value.

```
$isLoggedIn = $_SESSION["login"];

if ($isLoggedIn == 1){
// do something
}else{
// send back to login
}
```

You can use session_unset(); to remove everything that is in the session array as well as session_destroy(); to completely destroy the session. Bear in mind if you destroy the session you will have to restart the session after that making sure that nothing is been output to the browser yet or will generate an error.

```
session_start();

$xx = session_id();
$_SESSION ["username"] = $username;
$_SESSION ["login"] = 1;

session_unset();
session_destroy();
```

—

```
session_start();
$yy=session_id();
echo $xx;
echo "<br>";
echo $yy;
```

Sessions can expire.

The default for sessions is to keep a session open indefinitely and only to expire a session when the browser is closed. This can be changed in the php.ini file by altering the line
session.cookie_lifetime = 0
to a value in seconds. If you wanted the session to finish in 5 minutes you would set this to
session.cookie_lifetime = 300
and restart your httpd server.

Session info from PHP

Session Support __ enabled
Registered save handlers __ files user
Registered serializer handlers __ php_serialize php php_binary wddx

Directive	Local Value	Master Value
session.auto_start	Off	Off
session.cache_expire	180	180
session.cache_limiter	nocache	nocache
session.cookie_domain	no value	no value
session.cookie_httponly	Off	Off
session.cookie_lifetime	0	0
session.cookie_path	/	/
session.cookie_secure	Off	Off
session.entropy_file	no value	no value

```
session.entropy_length __ 0 __ 0
session.gc_divisor __ 100 __ 100
session.gc_maxlifetime __ 5440 __ 5440
session.gc_probability __ 1 __ 1
session.hash_bits_per_character __ 4 __ 4
session.hash_function __ 0 __ 0
session.name __ PHPSESSID __ PHPSESSID
session.referer_check __ no value __ no value
session.save_handler __ files __ files
session.save_path __ /data/tmp __ /data/tmp
session.serialize_handler __ php __ php
session.upload_progress.cleanup __ On __ On
session.upload_progress.enabled __ On __ On
session.upload_progress.freq __ 1% __ 1%
session.upload_progress.min_freq __ 1 __ 1
session.upload_progress.name __
PHP_SESSION_UPLOAD_PROGRESS __
PHP_SESSION_UPLOAD_PROGRESS
session.upload_progress.prefix __ upload_progress __
_upload_progress_
session.use_cookies __ On __ On
session.use_only_cookies __ On __ On
session.use_strict_mode __ Off __ Off
session.use_trans_sid __ 0 __ 0
```

As the above table shows this is all the information and use on this particular server dealing with sessions.

Our session timeout is set to session.cookie_lifetime = 0 which means technically it will not timeout. However various other things actually can timeout so it is up to you to keep track.

—

MYSQLI

Mysqli is not a function or command it is an extension to PHP , technically it represents a class thus you have to use the keyword new to call the class. Classes represent object orientated programming that allows you to utilize the entire object including all functions attached to it. At the end of this section you will see a complete list of all the callable functions attached to the mysqli class.

In this section we will only be looking at a few of the most pertinent things that you are likely to do.
note:
Mysql was deprecated as of php 5.5.0 and removed completly from php 7.0

For the MySQLi functions to be available, you must compile PHP with support for the MySQLi extension.

The MySQLi extension was introduced with PHP version 5.0.0. The MySQL Native Driver was included in PHP version 5.3.0.

In UNIX there are a variety of different databases that can be chosen however most servers in the world run just a few. MySql , MariaDB or Oracle. Through extensions to the PHP language, database access is relatively easy. PDO functions also allow database access with built-in security features diminishing the risk of SQL injection attacks. Through the proper coding practices MYSQLI can also perform at a higher level of security.

The main difference between MYSQL class and MYSQLI class is that you have to list the connection is part of the parameters necessary to access the database. The main advantage to this is being able to open up multiple databases at the same time because each will have its own unique connection ID.

Database access can be rather daunting for beginner in any language. If you're setting up the databases yourself, you have to follow the correct procedures including indexing to make all accessed items perform quickly. If your database only has a couple of tables and those tables have very few items then any calls to the database will be performed at a high rate of speed.

Generally the problem is when you databases become very large. You have 100 or so tables and some of the tables can have over 500,000 rows, performing queries on the database consumes a lot of processing power and access speed becomes retarded. This is where proper indexing can come to your rescue. You can reduce database access times from second's to milliseconds. It also reduces the load on the server and the database server. Whether you're server is MySql , MariaDB or Oracle, you have to remember it is a server similar to whatever servers running your webpages. Apache is the most common but there are others. It is necessary for the proper functioning of your server to have everything as streamlined as possible.

We will show you some of the basic commands to access data, then show you how to streamline those depending upon your needs.

MySqli Connect

First off, you have to make a connection to the server.
These examples present two different ways to build a connection.
The verse one builds basic connection and if it fails reports in error.

—

```
$con=mysqli_connect("localhost","my_user","my_password","m
y_db");
  // Check connection
  __ if (mysqli_connect_errno())
  __ {
  __ echo "Failed to connect to MySQL: " .
mysqli_connect_error();
  __ }
```

The second one also builds a connection but takes it one step
further and uses the die command if the connection fails and
then reports his much information about the errors possible.
The second one is also the preferred way as it clearly shows
you building the MYSQLII object class. You may notice the
keyword new.

```
$con = new mysqli($it_db_host, $it_db_user,
$it_db_pwd,$it_db_name); //connect to MySql
  __ if ($con->connect_error) {//Output any connection error
  __ die('Error : ('. $con->connect_errno .') '. $con-
>connect_error);
  __ }
```

Bear in mind that all errors should be dealt with in
preproduction of a website not after it is been fully launched.

Now assuming that your connection is fine, we can proceed
to make queries to the database.

Mysqli Query

Query examples.

// Perform queries

```
mysqli_query($con,"SELECT * FROM sometable");
mysqli_query($con,"INSERT INTO sometable
(FirstName,LastName,Age)
VALUES ('Scott','Newman',43)");
mysqli_close($con);
```

Those represent the basic structure of making a call or inserting data into the database. However they are somewhat incomplete.

```
$query = "select * from sometable where id ='$id' LIMIT 1";
$result = mysqli_query($con,$query) or die(mysqli_error($con)) ;
__ if(mysqli_num_rows($result)>=1)
__{
__ __ while ($getvalue = mysqli_fetch_array($result) )
__ __{
__ __ $tid=$getvalue["id"];
__ __ $name=$getvalue["name"];
__ __ // do something with the data
__ __}
__}
```

We have built the query string separately although we do not have to. Sometable represents the name of the table that we want to access and that name is case sensitive. In this case were selecting all from the database as denoted by the *. Using * represents all. We've also use the where word which tells it to look for something specific, in this case the row represented by the ID. We use single quotes around our variable $id because if we don't instead of using the variable you will treat it as a string. Any time in the query where you have an = and using a variable you need to use a single quotes around it.

$query = "select * from $mytable where id ='$id' LIMIT 1";

—

In the above query, $mytable is a variable but you do not use single quotes.

In the database the ID column is probably set to unique so we don't have to include LIMIT 1, however it is good practice to do so. The limit tells the query to only return the number of rows that the limit says.

The next line performs the actual query to the database.

$result = mysqli_query($con,$query) or die(mysqli_error($con)) ;

We are pushing whatever the query sends back into the variable $result that we will use later. The function mysqli_query($con,$query) has two parameters, the connection and the query. We then use the die command if for any reason there is a major error. The next line of code utilizes an if command to make sure that we have data.

if(mysqli_num_rows($result)>=1)

What were checking is the number of rows returned. If the number of rows is zero then we do not have any data so we do not perform any other tasks.

What we get returned is an array that contains all columns of that row or the ones that are specified only. In our example we've use the * or all so what is returned is every column of that particular role in the database.

while ($getvalue = mysqli_fetch_array($result))

Using the while command we will start extracting that data. Were setting a new variable called $getvalue to be used in our loop and the function mysqli_fetch_array($result)utilizes only one parameter are variable $result.

$tid=$getvalue["id"];
$name=$getvalue["name"];

The data returned is an array and as we loop through the array, in this case only once, we assign variables from the data received. The structure of the array is simple.

$getvalue["SomeColumnName"];

Utilizes the basic structure of an array, square brackets followed by either a string or we can actually use a variable.

$getvalue[$myColumn];

Strings have to be enclosed in double quotes or single quotes. Variables do not.

We have now assigned our variable $tid to whatever value is represented in that table row and column. This also applies to the variable $name.

Please note that we do not have to explicitly get the ID if we already have it but this is shown to illustrate various data that you can get from the database.

There are also ways to extract data from the database without knowing the names of the columns. This will be dealt with later in the book.

The syntax for putting data back into the database is slightly different.

If it is a new entry, you use INSERT, if it is an existing entry then you use UPDATE.

An example for insert.

INSERT INTO table_name (column1, column2, column3,...)
VALUES (value1, value2, value3,...)

$query = "Insert into sometable
(name,pass,name,email,joinDate,ip,token,atype)
VALUES('$name','$upassword','$username','$email','$tnow','$
testip','$token',1)";
$result = mysqli_query($con,$query) or die(mysqli_error($con));

—

We use parentheses for each part of the insert. The first part deals with the actual names of the columns in the database. The second part are the values that we want to insert. These must match in total so in the above example we are going to values for eight columns.
(name,pass,name,email,joinDate,ip,token,atype)

These represent the names of the columns.

We use the VALUES keyword for the next part to include the necessary data.
('$name','$upassword','$username','$email','$tnow','$testip','$token',1)";

Now most importantly is that the order matches so the first entry, name, must match the second part and in this case we are using a variable called $name. We also have to make sure that were matching the correct type of entry in the database because each column is assigned a type. NAME is assigned the type text.

Below are the storage limits for each type of TEXT and you have to make sure that you're also not exceeding those limits because it will produce an error or an irregular result.

☐TINYTEXT: 255 characters - 255 B. The TINYTEXT data object is the smallest of the TEXT family and is built to efficiently store short information strings. ...

☐TEXT: 65,535 characters - 64 KB. ...

☐MEDIUMTEXT: 16,777,215 - 16 MB. ...

☐LONGTEXT: 4,294,967,295 characters - 4 GB. .

In our case, the column called NAME could be tiny text and could easily fit a name. However is really important to understand your database structure to make sure that you understand what the columns are and what considerations you need to be aware of for your data

As can be seen from our example, we can use variables for the values or they can be set manually as in the case the last one using the numerical value 1. Because it is a numerical value is not necessary to use single quotes.

Integer values, similar to TEXT values have limits. Those are listed below

Type	Storage (Bytes)	Minimum Value (Signed/Unsigned)	Maximum Value (Signed/Unsigned)
TINYINT	1	-128	127
		0	255
SMALLINT	2	-32768	32767
		0	65535
MEDIUMINT	3	-8388608	8388607
		0	16777215
INT	4	-2147483648	2147483647
		0	4294967295
BIGINT	8	-9223372036854775808	9223372036854775807
		0	18446744073709551615

A complete list of all data types available for MySQL are available in the appendix section.

An example for UPDATE.

```
$query = "UPDATE sometable set lastLogin='$Lnow' where id ='$id' ";
$result = mysqli_query($con,$query) or die(mysqli_error($con)) ;
```

UPDATE utilizes the set keyword and follows the similar rules that you must assign a column and then a valued to updated . As well uses the where keyword and in this case we are working off the ID column.

—

```
$query = "UPDATE sometable set
lastLogin='$Lnow',usertoken='$newtoken' where id ='$id' ";
```

To update more than one column use a comma ,as a separator. For each one that you want to update, must be included in the list in the same format, column name value and then a, until you get to the last column that you want update and no further commas are used as a will actually generate an error.

Classes

We will be only touching on the absolute basics for classes. Searching Google will give you a multitude of tutorials on how to build and use classes. As well as PHPclasses.org offers a large variety of already created classes that you can use and or study to further your understanding of how classes work and how they can be utilized to streamline your code.

Classes are the basis for object orientated programming utilizing objects created from functions and data. Object-oriented programming has advantages over regular procedural style programming.
Most important is the do not repeat yourself principal that makes your code easier to maintain, modify and debug. Creating shorter code in less time with a higher degree of reusability.
Classes and objects are the main aspects of object orientated programming because a class is self-contained, contains all the independent variables and functions which work together forming a series of tasks.
In the most basic aspect they can be considered as a template from which a lot of different objects can be created.
A function always starts with the keyword <u>function</u> whereas classes start at the keyword <u>class</u>.
In a classic and have both public and private functions.

```
class boxes
{
// Declare properties
    public $length = 0;
    public $width = 0;

// Method to get the perimeter of the object
        public function getThePerimeter(){
        return (2 * ( $this-> length + $this-> width ));
        }
```

—

```
// Method to get the area of the object
    public function getTheArea(){
    return ( $this-> length * $this-> width );
    }
}
```

And this is how it can be used.
Classes should be kept in separate files making them more reusable than embedding them directly into your PHP code.

```
require "myclass.php";

// Create a new object from boxes class
$test = new boxes;

// Get the object properties values
echo $test-> length; // Output: 0
echo $test-> width; // Output: 0

// Set object properties values
$test -> length = 30;
$test -> width = 20;

// Read the object properties values again to show the
change
echo $test->length; // Output: 30
echo $test -> width; // Output: 20


// Call the object methods
echo $test-> getThePerimeter(); // Output: 100
echo $test-> getTheArea(); // Output: 600
```

You can make more than one object from the same code.

```
// Include class definition
require "myclass.php";

// Create multiple objects from the boxes class
$test1 = new boxes;
$test2 = new boxes;

// Call the methods of both the objects
echo $test1 -> getTheArea(); // Output: 0
echo $test2 -> getTheArea(); // Output: 0
```

```php
// Set $test1 properties values
$test1 -> length = 30;
$test1 -> width = 20;

// Set $test2 properties values
$test2 -> length = 35;
$test2 -> width = 50;

// Call the methods of both the objects again
echo $test1->getTheArea(); // Output: 600
echo $test2->getTheArea(); // Output: 1750
```

As well there are some extra keywords that can be utilized within a class. Construct and Extend.

```php
class person
    {
    // explicitly adding class properties are optional
- but
    // is good practice
    var $name;
    function __construct( $persons_name) {
    $this -> name = $persons_name;
    }

    public function get_name() {
    return $this -> name;
    }

    // protected methods and properties restrict access to
    // those elements.
    protected function set_name($new_name) {
    if ($this -> name != "Jimmy Two Fingers") {
        $this -> name = strtoupper($new_name);
    }
    }
    }

    // 'extends' is the keyword that enables inheritance
    class employee extends person
    {
    protected function set_name( $new_name) {
```

```php
    __    if ($new_name ==   "Stefan Beep") {
    __    $this -> name = $new_name;
    __    }
    __     else if ( $new_name ==   "Johnny Nounce") {
    __    person::set_name ( $new_name);
    __    }
    __    }

    __    function    __  construct ($employee_name)
    __    {
    __     __  $this -> set_name ( $employee_name);
    __    }
}
```

The construct keyword allows the class to initiate automatically in the extend keyword as extra function to the original class.

Notes: Using the symbol:

```
person::set_name ()
```

There is also a shortcut if you just want refer to current class's parent – by using the 'parent' keyword.

The code:

```php
protected function set_name ( $new_name )
{ __
    __    if ($new_name ==   "Stefan Beep") {
    __    $this-> name = $new_name; __
    __     }
    __     else if ($new_name ==   "Johnny Nounce") {
    __    parent::set_name ( $new_name ); __
    __     }
}
```

Some simple rules

Even with variable naming conventions, people tend to complicate it. There is absolutely no reason for this. At most you might save a couple extra bytes with the trade-off being that you have no idea what the variable is supposed to do. An example of this is writing a database access to display information contained within a database. The database perhaps has 15 different columns and say 4000 rows. Each row contains all the information pertaining to that entry across all 15 columns.

In the database you are likely to have a column called ID as this is a common practice for building databases because it gives you a unique reference to a given row. If the fifth column is used as a date reference, you can easily access that and pull the information that you want to display.

—

Now when accessing the database you wanted to be as memorable as possible so that you have a clear understanding of what the data is that you trying to retrieve. There are a variety of different ways that you can accomplish this. It can be converted to an object because it is already an array and then you can single step through the array and grab whatever details you want or you can simply grab the information on the fly and assign it to a variable. Most likely this is how you going to get the data. Now it makes no sense whatsoever to use a variable that doesn't somehow reflect the name of the column or the data contained within that column. Using a convention of $X1 through $X15 will work however now you have to remember what each one is both represent so the most easiest way is the name your variable in such a way that it reflects what the data is, in this case a date. So perhaps it is the last time the visitor was on the website. In that case perhaps the best variable would be $LastOnDate. In this way gives you a pretty good indication of what the variable is being used for. As well you may have noticed that we mixed upper and lower case in this particular variable. That is purely for readability however I have to point out that on a UNIX server, which most of the world runs on, upper and lowercase can mean entirely different things and $lastondate is not the same as $LastOnDate. In fact UNIX will treat it as an entirely new variable.

There will be more on databases further along in the book. What I am attempting to here is just give you a basic understanding of some of the concepts being presented.

Most people that is just starting out and PHP, have seen the basic example of writing something on the screen or webpage as the case may be. This is the classic hello world that almost all programming languages utilize as starting point. I will assume that you've already check that out however here is the basic concept.

```
<html>
```

```
<head>
<title>PHP Test</title>
</head>
<body>
<?php echo '<p>Hello World</p>';?>
</body>
</html>
```

As you can see, you can freely mix PHP and HTML together. This is not an absolute requirement but useful in most cases.

A simple rule is that in order for it to be a PHP page and be interpreted correctly the file name must end in .php so an example would be, mywebpage.php.

—

Reusable pages

One of the most important aspects in designing websites is you want everything to match a given structure and layout. A lot of times people will write the same code in every page of the website when this is absolutely unnecessary. As well it makes it incredibly difficult to make changes because now you have to make a change in every single page on the website to reflect the differences.

When we design a website, we generally start with three basic files.

Pre-header
header
footer

Contained within the pre-header generally is the pure PHP that is responsible for something such as attaching to a database, assigning global variables. Cookies and tracking as well as other details.

The header generally contains all her basic CSS information so that all webpages on the site will be identical.

The footer generally contains all the other bits as well as a lot of times the actual JavaScript being utilized and copyright information. As well in the footer, site maps and other useful information may be contained as well.

PHP itself makes it easy for you to include pages in any webpage.

If we have a file called index.php it may contain something like this

```
<?
include('preheader.php');
$pageid1=1;
```

```
include('header.php');

$filelocation=$themedir."indexd.php";

include($filelocation);


include('footer.php');
?>
```
This represents the entirety of the index.php file.

As you can see, it's pulling in a variety of different files to be able to display the page properly as a webpage.

In the pre-header file we have a variable called $themedir.

This is one of the variables that is been set in the pre-header, know whether or not it got the information from a database or text file, it sets a directory for which the files being pulled from. Often times in a website you have a directory specifically designed to hold the current theme. Word press uses this concept always.

An example of the preheader file

```
<?
session_start();

$debugON=0;
if ($debugON==1){
ini_set('display_errors', 1);
ini_set('display_startup_errors', 1);
error_reporting(E_ALL);
}
include('track.php');
setlocale(LC_MONETARY,"en_US"); // US national format
(see : http://php.net/money_format)
```

—

```php
if ( isset ($_SESSION["ip"])){
}else{
global $testip;
if ( isset ($_SERVER["HTTP_X_FORWARDED"])){
$testip = $_SERVER["HTTP_X_FORWARDED"];
}elseif ( isset ($_SERVER["HTTP_FORWARDED_FOR"])){
$testip = $_SERVER["HTTP_FORWARDED_FOR"];
}elseif ( isset ($_SERVER["HTTP_FORWARDED"])){
$testip = $_SERVER["HTTP_FORWARDED"];
}elseif ( isset ($_SERVER["HTTP_X_FORWARDED"])){
$testip = $_SERVER["HTTP_X_FORWARDED"];
}else{
if ( isset ($_SERVER["REMOTE_ADDR"])){
$testip = $_SERVER["REMOTE_ADDR"];}
}
$_SESSION["ip"]=$testip;

}

global $con;
include('config.php');
$con = new mysqli($db_host, $db_username,
$db_password,$db_name); //connect to MySql
if ($con->connect_error) {//Output any connection error
die('Error : ('. $con->connect_errno .') '. $con->connect_error);
}
include('getSettings.php');
include('functions/sitefunctions.php');
?>
```

Okay let's start breaking apart the page to see what each bit does.

Setting the session variable is a handy way to pass data from page to page in one of the only prerequisites is that it should be the very first line in the script.

Using session variables is extremely efficient at passing hidden data and something that you should consider using. Once a user is submitted a form and/or logged in, or something similar you want an easy way to maintain the data.

Debug mode.

In preproduction of your webpages you want to try and catch as many errors as you can but once the website is up and fully functional what you don't want is to have those errors showing up on the pages. There are different ways to handle errors including emailing bug reports to yourself. An examples will be in a later chapter.

Simply speaking we set up variable to tell if you want to use debug mode. If the variable equals one then all errors will be displayed.

Were using and include statement call track.php and possibly in that file is a collection of various information including the use of cookies and other code.

Setlocale

this is a PHP command that sets in this case, the currency that we want to use on the website. Very handy if this is an e-commerce site. We can dynamically adjust the locale depending upon what country the person is from.

TESTIP

First off the browser provides a wealth of information including the actual IP address that your visitors coming from. However occasionally some people will try and hide that particular information in a variety of different ways.

First off we check to see if our session variable is already set and if it is, we just continue because we already have the IP address.

If is a very powerful command and allows us to apply various levels of logic to the code to see if something is true or not.

—

In this case, if the session variable is not set, we start stepping through the list of possibilities to acquire the correct IP address. Once that is complete we then set the session variable.

Next we set up another global variable to use as their connection to a database. $con is the variable were going to use and the main reason for setting the global is so that we can use it in functions at a later time. We next need to acquire or database information that we stored in another file called config.php. This is simply a text file with our variables preset.
$con = new mysqli($db_host, $db_username, $db_password,$db_name);

MySqli is the recommended command to use the older version, Mysql , is being phased out completely and no longer available in PHP 7. It is also more secure than the older version.

Our variable $con will contain the necessary connection information so that we can now open the database to retrieve data. This particular command takes four variables.

HOST - usually this is localhost however depending on where you are hosting your website they may use something different.

USERNAME- username is a requirement for the database itself and has been assigned to the database by whatever server level system is in charge of the databases.

PASSWORD- once again this is been assigned by the server level system that is in charge of the databases.

DATABASE NAME- this is the actual database itself and not the name of the table in the database.

If all the information is correct an error will not be produced but if there is an error we have that covered with
if ($con->connect_error) {//Output any connection error

die('Error : ('. $con->connect_errno .') '. $con->connect_error);

}

this particular statement. In the event of an error, it will display as much possible information about that error. Most likely an error will occur if the username or password is not absolutely correct. If you get an error, then you need to check the details and make whatever correction is necessary. We've included the die command which effectively stops the script entirely. The main reason for this is that if you can't connect to the database, and you need to connect to database to display information than is no point going forward until that error been corrected.

The next two includes bring in any other information that we want as well as including all the prewritten functions that we will be using.

Note:

Be aware that any output of any kind including echo statements, print statements, error statements will produce an error on their own if that occurs before your header statement is sent out.

An example of a header statement.

```
<!doctype html>
<!--[if IE 9]><html class="lt-ie10" lang="en" > <![endif]-->
<html class="no-js" lang="en" data-useragent="Mozilla/5.0
(compatible; MSIE 10.0; Windows NT 6.2; Trident/6.0)">
    <head>
    <meta charset="utf-8" />
    <meta name="viewport" content="width=device-width,
initial-scale=1.0" />


    <meta name="description" content="MY Great Site." />

    <meta name="author" content="Independent Technical" />
```

—

```
<meta name="copyright" content="<?=$sitename?> (c)2018"
/>
  <link rel="stylesheet" href="css/normalize.css">
  <link rel="stylesheet" href="css/foundation.css" />
  <link rel="stylesheet" href="css/panels.css" />
  <link rel="stylesheet" href="css/extra.css" />

  </head>
```

Now even if your website as a few hundred pages, using this method to include all the information and CSS, making changes can be accomplished quickly and easily. The main goal is to have your website have a consistent look and feel. Including all the same code in every page is not an efficient way to do things. Putting together your website in such a way that it utilizes the same code across multiple pages not only save you time coding but also makes it easier to fix errors.

Reusable code

Over the course of many years programming I have always looked at ways to streamline the process. There is no point in writing every algorithm from scratch or creating new functions when it isn't necessary.

Once you have a function perfected you can probably make it generic enough to be used anywhere you like. An example.

```
function monthDay($timestring){
$humandate = date("M j",$timestring);
return $humandate;
}
function fulldate($timestring){
$humandate = date("F j, Y, g:i a",$timestring);
return $humandate;
}
```

These are couple of very simple date functions. You of course can also do it in one line code.

```
$humandate = date("M j",$timestring);
```

However once you've built up a library of date functions, it is far more efficient to include those functions and then call whichever one you have need of it the time. Now the date function itself can get fairly complicated if you want. Rarely is there a need for that but there are specialized commands that can be utilized.

From the manual:

FORMAT

—

The format of the outputted date string. See the formatting options below. There are also several predefined date constants that may be used instead, so for example DATE_RSS contains the format string 'D, d M Y H:i:s'.

The following characters are recognized in the format parameter string

format character __ Description __ Example returned values

Day __ --- __ ---

d __ Day of the month, 2 digits with leading zeros __ 01 to 31

D __ A textual representation of a day, three letters __ Mon through Sun

j __ Day of the month without leading zeros __ 1 to 31

l (lowercase 'L') __ A full textual representation of the day of the week __ Sunday through Saturday

N __ ISO-8601 numeric representation of the day of the week (added in PHP 5.1.0) __ 1 (for Monday) through 7 (for Sunday)

S __ English ordinal suffix for the day of the month, 2 characters __ st, nd, rd or th. Works well with j

w __ Numeric representation of the day of the week __ 0 (for Sunday) through 6 (for Saturday)

z __ The day of the year (starting from 0) __ 0 through 365

Week __ --- __ ---

W __ ISO-8601 week number of year, weeks starting on Monday __ Example: 42 (the 42nd week in the year)

Month __ --- __ ---

F __ A full textual representation of a month, such as January or March __ January through December

m __ Numeric representation of a month, with leading zeros __ 01 through 12

M __ A short textual representation of a month, three letters __ Jan through Dec

n __ Numeric representation of a month, without leading zeros __ 1 through 12

t __ Number of days in the given month __ 28 through 31

Year __ --- __ ---

L __ Whether it's a leap year __ 1 if it is a leap year, 0 otherwise.

o __ ISO-8601 week-numbering year. This has the same value as Y, except that if the ISO week number (W) belongs to the previous or next year, that year is used instead. (added in PHP 5.1.0) __ Examples: 1999 or 2003

Y __ A full numeric representation of a year, 4 digits __ Examples: 1999 or 2003

y __ A two digit representation of a year __ Examples: 99 or 03

Time __ --- __ ---

a __ Lowercase Ante meridiem and Post meridiem __ am or pm

A __ Uppercase Ante meridiem and Post meridiem __ AM or PM

B __ Swatch Internet time __ 000 through 999

g __ 12-hour format of an hour without leading zeros __ 1 through 12

G __ 24-hour format of an hour without leading zeros __ 0 through 23

h __ 12-hour format of an hour with leading zeros __ 01 through 12

H __ 24-hour format of an hour with leading zeros __ 00 through 23

i __ Minutes with leading zeros __ 00 to 59

s __ Seconds, with leading zeros __ 00 through 59

u __ Microseconds (added in PHP 5.2.2). Note that date() will always generate 000000 since it takes an integer parameter, whereas DateTime::format() does support microseconds if DateTime was created with microseconds. __ Example: 654321

v __ Milliseconds (added in PHP 7.0.0). Same note applies as for u. __ Example: 654

Timezone __ --- __ ---

e __ Timezone identifier (added in PHP 5.1.0) __ Examples: UTC, GMT, Atlantic/Azores

—

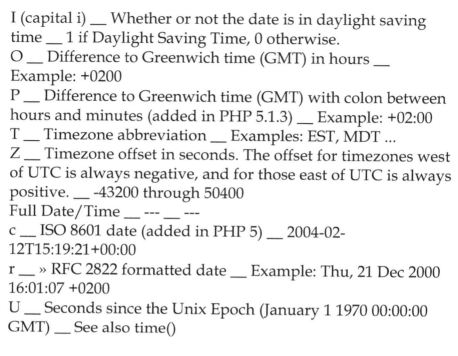

I (capital i) __ Whether or not the date is in daylight saving time __ 1 if Daylight Saving Time, 0 otherwise.

O __ Difference to Greenwich time (GMT) in hours __ Example: +0200

P __ Difference to Greenwich time (GMT) with colon between hours and minutes (added in PHP 5.1.3) __ Example: +02:00

T __ Timezone abbreviation __ Examples: EST, MDT ...

Z __ Timezone offset in seconds. The offset for timezones west of UTC is always negative, and for those east of UTC is always positive. __ -43200 through 50400

Full Date/Time __ --- __ ---

c __ ISO 8601 date (added in PHP 5) __ 2004-02-12T15:19:21+00:00

r __ » RFC 2822 formatted date __ Example: Thu, 21 Dec 2000 16:01:07 +0200

U __ Seconds since the Unix Epoch (January 1 1970 00:00:00 GMT) __ See also time()

With all the options available, the best programming practice would be to build a library of date functions that become reusable in all of your development work.

When building functions, it is best to group all functions of the same purpose, in the same file. An example of this would be dates.php. Then you simply include the file wherever it is needed.

Generic functions

For any given website, you're likely to make a whole bunch of different functions that are pertinent to that website and only that website. What this really means is that you have to rewrite your functions again for different site. There are ways to make a generic so that you only have to write the function once you can reuse it.

Consider this example. It makes a call to the database to retrieve some information that is pertinent to that particular database and table.

```
function getName($pid){
global $con;
$sql="SELECT * FROM user where id='$pid' limit 1";
 $rsM = mysqli_query($con,$sql) or die(mysqli_error($con)
);
 $count = mysqli_num_rows($rsM);
 if ($count >= 1){
while($row = $rsM->fetch_assoc()) {


$Tuname=$row["uName"];
}
return $Tuname;

}else{
return 0;
}
}
```

Now make it generic
we are going to select from the table where we already know the ID number for the row.

```
function getTable($table,$column,$pid){
```

—

```
    global $con;
    $sql="SELECT * FROM $table where id='$pid' limit 1";
    $rsM = mysqli_query($con,$sql) or die(mysqli_error($con)
);
    $count = mysqli_num_rows($rsM);
    if ($count >= 1){
    while($row = $rsM->fetch_assoc()) {


    $Tvar=$row[$column];
    }
    return $Tvar;

    }else{
    return 0;
    }
    }
```

As you can see, the new function performs an almost identical role with the exception that you supply the table name and the column name that you want.

```
    $myname= getTable('user','uname',$pid);
```

We have use single quotes around the names that we are looking for however they can also be a predefined variable.

Any of your existing functions can probably be converted in very similar manner.

Making a more complex function is still as easy.

```
    function getRow($table,$id){
    global $con;
    $results = mysqli_query($con,"SELECT * FROM $table
where id='$id' limit 1");
    $count = mysqli_num_rows($results);
```

```
if ($count >= 1){
// set array
$array = array();
// look through query
while($row = mysqli_fetch_assoc($query)){
// add entire row returned into an array
$array[] = $row;
return $array;
}
}else{
return 0;
}
}
```

That will return the entire row from the database but we can do even more by adding a bit to the function by using the LIKE command

```
function getAllRows($table,$column,$name,$tlimit){
global $con;
$results = mysqli_query($con,"SELECT * FROM $table
where $column LIKE '%$name%' limit $tlimit");
$count = mysqli_num_rows($results);
if ($count >= 1){
// set array
$array = array();
// look through query
while($row = mysqli_fetch_assoc($results)){
// add entire row returned into an array
$array[] = $row;

}
return $array;
}else{
return 0;
}
```

—

```
}
```

WE would call the function like this.

```
$table="products";
$column="productname";
$name="ballon";
$out=getAllRows($table,$column,$name,2);

echo "<pre>";
print_r($out);
echo "</pre>";
```

Of course that will just simply dump the data to the screen and to make real use of the data we need to step through the array and extract whatever pertinent information is necessary. This is an example of what the dump will look like.

```
Array
(
[0] => Array
(
[id] => 1
[edate] => 1419861393
[sku] => sp0011438241352
[productname] => Love Forever After
[productType] => 0
[usevars] => 0
[ptype1] => 75
[ptype2] => 0
[specs] =>
[price] => 2.99
[listprice] => 0
[image] => u_1396404648after.png
[featured] => 0
[sale] => 0
```

[newproduct] => 0
[stock] => 0
[shippingitem] => 0
[taxexempt] => 0
[active] => 1
[views] => 0
[supplier] => 0
[cost] => 0
[reorder] => 0
[sold] => 0
[spbn] => 0011438241352
[pviews] => 0
)

[1] => Array
(
[id] => 6
[edate] => 1419860105
[sku] => sp0011438395484
[productname] => Love by Dawn
[productType] => 0
[usevars] => 0
[ptype1] => 75
[ptype2] => 0
[specs] =>
[price] => 2.99
[listprice] => 0
[image] => u_1457319262-new-500.jpg
[featured] => 0
[sale] => 0
[newproduct] => 0
[stock] => 0
[shippingitem] => 0
[taxexempt] => 0
[active] => 1
[views] => 0

—

```
[supplier] => 0
[cost] => 0
[reorder] => 0
[sold] => 0
[spbn] => 0011438241352
[pviews] => 0
)
```

This particular function can be even made more robust by adding more to it. You can turn it into a general purpose function just by setting various conditional statements as part of the function itself.

By adding the switch statement to the function, you can now for more than one task.

```
function
getAllRows($table,$column,$name,$pid,$mtype,$tlimit){
  global $con;
  switch ($mtype){
  case 1:
  // get all information from one row
  $results = mysqli_query($con,"SELECT * FROM $table
where id='$pid' limit 1");
  break;
  case 2:
  // get all records matching search
  $results = mysqli_query($con,"SELECT * FROM $table
where $column LIKE '%$name%' limit $tlimit");
  break;
  }
  $count = mysqli_num_rows($results);
  if ($count >= 1){
  // set array
  $array = array();
  // look through query
```

```php
while($row = mysqli_fetch_assoc($results)){
// add entire row returned into an array
$array[] = $row;

}
return $array;
}else{
return 0;
  }
}
```

Using this particular method you can keep modifying your functions to perform more tasks efficiently. These particular examples are merely for illustrative purposes but they do convey the process.

—

HTML with PHP

It is quite easy, to freely mix HTML code with PHP. There is no particular reason to separate them.

In functions one of the main issues is that they will only return one thing, be that a variable for an array. However any function is capable of outputting HTML code.

```
<?

function getInfo($bid){
global $con;
$sql="SELECT * FROM sometable where bid='$bid' limit 1 ";
$result = mysqli_query($con,$sql) or die(mysqli_error() );
$count = mysqli_num_rows($rsM);
if ($count >= 1){
//we have data to use;
while ($rowM = mysqli_fetch_assoc($result))
{
// get all the information you need from the database
$id=$rowM['id'];
$image=$rowM['id'];
$edate=$rowM['edate'];
$title=$rowM['title'];
 $blurb=$rowM['blurb'];
 // NOW WE MIX IN THE HTML
?>
<article class="grid-container">
<div class="grid-x grid-margin-x">
 <div class="medium-4 cell">
 <img alt="image name" longdesc="imagename this site"
src="img/<?=$image?>">
 </div>
 <div class="medium-8 cell">
 <div class="callout primary center">
```

```
<div class="text-center">
<h4> <?=$title?></h4>

</div>
<div class="text-right">
<?=$blurb?>
</div>
</div>
</div>
</div>
</article>
<?
} // end while ($rowM = mysqli_fetch_assoc($result))
}// end if ($count >= 1){
}
?>
```

As you can see from the code, we would open the database and extracted the information and instead of sending back an array, we have opted to just output the information to the webpage.

Were incorporating CSS to display the data. In this case we are using one of the newer versions of Foundation but the same can be accomplished by using Bootstrap. Both of these frameworks are excellent at making mobile friendly webpages which are now required by Google.

To include HTML directly in the function we have used opening and closing PHP tags as this is the simplest way to do it. You can also echo or print each statement so that it is pure PHP. That method will also work but becomes more complicated and sometimes less readable.

```
echo "<article class='grid-container'>";
```
On of the most important rules here when using **Echo** or **Print** statements, is single and double quotes.

This can also be written like this.

—

```
echo 'article class="grid-container"'>'
```

This keeps it more in line without HTML is structured because in HTML it only uses double quotes.

You have to pay particular attention and make sure that you using the right type of quote symbols.

This is the main reason for choosing opening and closing tags instead.

The advantage of adding HTML code to this particular routine is that it also allows you to display things differently depending on given criteria.

Let's say in the database, a particular entry doesn't have an image so we can use an IF statement to modify our output.

```
<?
function getInfo($bid){
$sql="SELECT * FROM sometable where bid='$bid' limit 1 ";
$result = mysqli_query($con,$sql) or die(mysqli_error() );
$count = mysqli_num_rows($rsM);
if ($count >= 1){
//we have data to use;
while ($rowM = mysqli_fetch_assoc($result))
{
// get all the information you need from the database
$id=$rowM['id'];
$image=$rowM['id'];
$edate=$rowM['edate'];
$title=$rowM['title'];
 $blurb=$rowM['blurb'];
 // NOW WE MIX IN THE HTML
?>

<article class="grid-container">
<div class="grid-x grid-margin-x">
<?
if ($image=""){
```

```
?>

<div class="medium-12 cell">
<div class="callout primary center">
<div class="text-center">
<h4> <?=$title?></h4>

</div>
<div class="text-right">
<?=$blurb?>
</div>
</div>
</div>

<?
}ELSE{
?>
  <div class="medium-4 cell">
  <img alt="image name" longdesc="imagename this site"
src="img/<?=$image?>">
  </div>
  <div class="medium-8 cell">
  <div class="callout primary center">
  <div class="text-center">
  <h4> <?=$title?></h4>

</div>
<div class="text-right">
<?=$blurb?>
</div>
</div>
</div>
<?
}
?>
```

—

```
</div>
</article>
<?
} // end while ($rowM = mysqli_fetch_assoc($result))
}// end if ($count >= 1){
}
?>
```

You can add whatever decision-making you need into the function depending upon what and how you want things displayed.

Of course there is embedding directly into your code if what you want to do is a one off. Using a function generally means that on any given page, you going to be calling that function more than once. Here's an example of embedded code .

```
<?
$query = "select * from sometable where word ='$tword'";
$result = mysqli_query($con,$query) or
die(mysqli_error($con)) ;
if(mysqli_num_rows($resultSub)>=1)
{
//$output[];
while ($getvalue = mysqli_fetch_array($result) )
{
$id=$getvalue["id"];
$key=$getvalue["word"];
$ttype=trim($getvalue["ttype"]);
$syn=$getvalue["syn"];
if ($syn<>""){
$esyn=explode(",",$syn);
sort($esyn, SORT_NATURAL);
$syno="";
foreach ($esyn as $value) {
$syno .=trim($value) .", ";
}
```

```php
$syn=$syno;
}
$ant=$getvalue["tant"];
if ($ant<>""){
$eant=explode(",",$ant);
sort($eant, SORT_NATURAL);
$syno="";
foreach ($eant as $value) {
$anto .=trim($value) .", ";
}
$ant=$anto;
}

if ($ttype<>""){
//echo $ttype."<br>";
switch ($ttype){
case "-n":
echo $ttype." Noun <br>";
break;
case "-v":
echo $ttype." Verb <br>";
break;
case "-adj":
echo $ttype." Adjective <br>";
break;
case "-a":
echo $ttype." Adjective <br>";
break;
case "-prep":
echo $ttype." Preposition <br>";
break;
case "-adv":
echo $ttype." Adverb <br>";
break;
}
}
```

—

```
//echo $tsyn."<br>";
//echo $tant."<br>";
?>
<div class="callout secondary">
<center>SYN</center><br>
<?=$syn?>
</div>
<div class="callout success">
<center>ANT</center><br>
<?=$ant?>
</div>
<?
}
}else{
// nothing found
// echo "Nothing Found";
echo $_POST['word']. " not Found";
}

?>
```

This example clearly illustrates some of the ways the mix HTML and PHP code.

Now the downside of mixing the PHP and HTML in a function is that it makes it harder to make it reusable and tends to be an one off for a website. It is not impossible to create it as reusable code as long as the css and the database are the same or similar.

CSS and PHP

Usually CSS is hardcoded. Large libraries of CSS code as frameworks such as Foundation and Bootstrap have thousands of lines of code as well as all the necessary JavaScript to make it all work smoothly.

Manually going through each line of code to make changes is tedious especially if you have to do this for every website that your building.

It is possible with PHP to create the given files to set such things as colour, fonts and more. It is somewhat more difficult but doable.

Perhaps the best way is to create the scripts that will set the colours and then re-create the CSS files.

Currently we are working with Foundation 643 and have created the code to do just that. It takes many hours to go through each section of the code looking for ways to embed a variable for colour. The end result is worth it because now all the necessary routines to make major colour changes that become usable on any new website. A customized CSS file is created as an end result of that. What is being utilized is a small PHP file that all the colour choices are located in and then process all the CSS files together into one.

I won't put all the code and here, but enough to give you general idea of how you can do yourself.

—

What we do first is make a copy of the foundation CSS file and then work with a particular copy. Next we cut pertinent sections from that CSS file and put them in a new CSS file with a PHP extension. After we have broken it into all the sections that we require, it is time to build a code for setting the colours for each section. Using foundation, tabs for each section seems to work the best. You can add the colour changing code on each section in each tab, make all the changes you require to the colour processing page that will create the necessary PHP CSS file. Once you've rebuilt all the sections using dynamic created colours. You can then merge the final results into one large CSS file.

We will be building a file called colours.php and this would be created dynamically.

This particular example is for creating different background panel colours texts etc.

Please note that this is part of a larger program.

```
<div class = "grid-container">
<div class = "large-16 small-16 cell ">

<div class = "grid-x grid-padding-x">

<h4>Save it</h4><br>
<input name = "doitColours" type = "hidden" value = "1">
<input class = "button expanded round" name = "Submit1" type = "submit" value = " Save " />

<div class = "large-4 small-12 cell"><!-- class=12 colums main part of page-->
<?
// id panel theme linkcolour vlinkcolour hlinkcolourbodycolour bodyimage logolarge logosmall mainpageblurb tagline logoimage shippingpage aboutpage
?>
```

```
<div class = "callout ">
<center>
Body Colour<br>
<input name = "bodycolour" type = "hidden" id = "body_value"
value = "<? = $bodycolour?>" />
<button class = "small button expanded jscolor {valueElement:
'body_value'}">Pick a color</button>
Body Text<br>
<input name = "bodytext" type = "hidden" id = "bodytext_value"
value = "<? = $bodytext?>" />
<button class = "small button expanded jscolor {valueElement:
'bodytext_value'}">Pick a color</button>
Link Colour<br>
<input name = "linkcolour" type = "hidden" id = "link_value"
value = "<? = $linkcolour?>" />
<button class = "small button expanded jscolor {valueElement:
'link_value'}">Pick a color</button>
Hover Link Colour<br>
<input name = "hlinkcolour" type = "hidden" id = "hlink_value"
value = "<? = $hlinkcolour?>" />
<button class = "small button expanded jscolor {valueElement:
'hlink_value'}">Pick a color</button>
Visited Link<br>
<input name = "vlinkcolour" type = "hidden" id = "vlink_value"
value="<? = $vlinkcolour?>" />
<button class = "small button expanded jscolor {valueElement:
'vlink_value'}">Pick a color</button>
Standard Callout/Panel
</center>
</div>
</div>
<div class = "large-4 small-12 cell"><!-- class=12 columns main
part of page-->
<div class = "callout ">
Panels/Callout<br>
Standard <br>
BackGround Colour <br>
```

—

```
<input name = "calloutbgcolour" type = "hidden" id =
"calloutbgcolour_value" value="<? = $calloutbgcolour?>" />
<button class = "small button expanded jscolor {valueElement:
'calloutbgcolour_value'}">Pick a color</button>
Border Color<br>
<input name = "calloutborder" type = "hidden" id =
"calloutborder_value" value = "<? = $calloutborder?>" />
<button class = "small button expanded jscolor {valueElement:
'calloutborder_value'}">Pick a color</button>
Callout Text<br>
<input name = "callouttext" type = "hidden" id =
"callouttext_value" value = "<? = $callouttext?>" />
<button class = "small button expanded jscolor {valueElement:
'callouttext_value'}">Pick a color</button>
<hr>
Standard Callout/Panel
<h4>HeaderText</h4>
</div></div>
<div class = "large-4 small-12 cell"><!-- class=12 colums main
part of page-->
<div class = "callout primary">
Panels/Callout<br>
Primary <br>
BackGround Colour <br>
<input name = "calloutbgcolourp" type = "hidden" id =
"calloutbgcolourp_value" value = "<? = $calloutbgcolourp?>" />
<button class = "small button expanded jscolor {valueElement:
'calloutbgcolourp_value'}">Pick a color</button>
Border Color<br>
<input name = "calloutborderp" type = "hidden" id =
"calloutborderp_value" value = "<? = $calloutborderp?>" />
<button class = "small button expanded jscolor {valueElement:
'calloutborderp_value'}">Pick a color</button>
Callout Text<br>
<input name = "callouttextp" type = "hidden" id =
"callouttextp_value" value = "<? = $callouttextp?>" />
```

```
<button class = "small button expanded jscolor {valueElement:
'callouttextp_value'}">Pick a color</button>
<hr>
Primary Callout/Panel
<h4>HeaderText</h4>
</div></div>
<div class = "large-4 small-12 cell"><!-- class=12 colums main
part of page-->
<div class = "callout secondary">
Panels/Callout<br>
Secondary <br>
BackGround Colour <br>
<input name = "calloutbgcolours" type = "hidden" id =
"calloutbgcolours_value" value = "<? = $calloutbgcolours?>" />
<button class = "small button expanded jscolor {valueElement:
'calloutbgcolours_value'}">Pick a color</button>
Border Color<br>
<input name = "calloutborders" type = "hidden" id =
"calloutborders_value" value = "<? = $calloutborders?>" />
<button class = "small button expanded jscolor {valueElement:
'calloutborders_value'}">Pick a color</button>
Callout Text<br>
<input name = "callouttexts" type = "hidden" id =
"callouttexts_value" value = "<? = $callouttexts?>" />
<button class = "small button expanded jscolor {valueElement:
'callouttexts_value'}">Pick a color</button>
<hr>
Secondary Callout/Panel
<h4>HeaderText</h4>
</div></div>
<div class = "large-4 small-12 cell"><!-- class=12 colums main
part of page-->
<div class = "callout alert">
Panels/Callout<br>
Alert <br>
BackGround Colour <br>
```

—

```
<input name = "calloutbgcoloura" type = "hidden" id =
"calloutbgcoloura_value" value = "<? = $calloutbgcoloura?>" />
<button class = "small button expanded jscolor {valueElement:
'calloutbgcoloura_value'}">Pick a color</button>
Border Color<br>
<input name = "calloutbordera" type = "hidden" id =
"calloutbordera_value" value = "<? = $calloutbordera?>" />
<button class = "small button expanded jscolor {valueElement:
'calloutbordera_value'}">Pick a color</button>
Callout Text<br>
<input name = "callouttexta" type = "hidden" id =
"callouttexta_value" value = "<? = $callouttexta?>" />
<button class = "small button expanded jscolor {valueElement:
'callouttexta_value'}">Pick a color</button>
<hr>
Alert Callout/Panel
<h4>HeaderText</h4>
</div></div>
<div class = "large-4 small-12 cell">
<div class = "callout success">
Panels/Callout<br>
Success <br>
BackGround Colour <br>
<input name = "calloutbgcolourss" type = "hidden" id =
"calloutbgcolourss_value" value = "<? = $calloutbgcolourss?>" />
<button class = "small button expanded jscolor {valueElement:
'calloutbgcolourss_value'}">Pick a color</button>
Border Color<br>
<input name = "calloutborderss" type = "hidden" id =
"calloutborderss_value" value = "<? = $calloutborderss?>" />
<button class = "small button expanded jscolor {valueElement:
'calloutborderss_value'}">Pick a color</button>
Callout Text<br>
<input name = "callouttextss" type = "hidden" id =
"callouttextss_value" value = "<? = $callouttextss?>" />
<button class = "small button expanded jscolor {valueElement:
'callouttextss_value'}">Pick a color</button>
```

```
<hr>
Success Callout/Panel
<h4>HeaderText</h4>
</div></div>
 </div>
 </div>
 </div>
```

We use an Ajax colour picker to set or assign different colour values to each section.

Once we've set all the colours, we save it and then process the file.

```
<?
if ( isset ($_POST ['doitColours'])){
/*
$bodycolour = "#FFFFFF";
$linkcolour = "000000";
$hlinkcolour = "000000";
$vlinkcolour = "000000";
*/
$bodycolour = $_POST ['bodycolour'];
$bodytext = $_POST ['bodytext'];
$linkcolour = $_POST ['linkcolour'];
$hlinkcolour = $_POST ['hlinkcolour'];
$vlinkcolour = $_POST ['vlinkcolour'];
$topbarbackgroundcolour = $_POST ['topbarbackgroundcolour'];
$topbartextcolour = $_POST ['topbartextcolour'];
//panels
$calloutbgcolour = $_POST ['calloutbgcolour'];
$callouttext = $_POST ['callouttext'];
$calloutborder = $_POST ['calloutborder'];
$calloutbgcolourp = $_POST ['calloutbgcolourp'];
$callouttextp = $_POST ['callouttextp'];
$calloutborderp = $_POST ['calloutborderp'];
```

—

```php
$calloutbgcolours = $_POST ['calloutbgcolours'];
$callouttexts = $_POST ['callouttexts'];
$calloutborders = $_POST ['calloutborders'];
$calloutbgcoloura = $_POST ['calloutbgcoloura'];
$callouttexta = $_POST ['callouttexta'];
$calloutbordera = $_POST ['calloutbordera'];
$calloutbgcolourss = $_POST ['calloutbgcolourss'];
$callouttextss = $_POST ['callouttextss'];
$calloutborderss = $_POST ['calloutborderss'];
// buttons standard
$buttonbg = $_POST ['buttonbg'];
$buttonbgh = $_POST ['buttonbgh'];
$buttonborder = $_POST ['buttonborder'];
$buttontext = $_POST ['buttontext'];
$buttontexth = $_POST ['buttontexth'];
$buttonbgdis = $_POST ['buttonbgdis'];
// buttons primary
$buttonbgp = $_POST ['buttonbgp'];
$buttonbghp = $_POST ['buttonbghp'];
$buttonborderp = $_POST ['buttonborderp'];
$buttontextp = $_POST ['buttontextp'];
$buttontexthp = $_POST ['buttontexthp'];
$buttonbgdisp = $_POST ['buttonbgdisp'];

// buttons secondary
$buttonbgs = $_POST ['buttonbgs'];
$buttonbghs = $_POST ['buttonbghs'];
$buttonborders = $_POST ['buttonborders'];
$buttontexts = $_POST ['buttontexts'];
$buttontexths = $_POST ['buttontexths'];
$buttonbgdiss = $_POST ['buttonbgdiss'];



//----------------------------------------------------------------
----


$myfile=fopen ($ccopy, "w") or die("Unable to open file!");
```

```php
// opening php statement
$txt="<" . "?" . "\n";
fwrite ($myfile, $txt);
// $ var name = var then newline
$txt="$" . "bodycolour = " . "'#" . $bodycolour . "';" . "\n";
fwrite ($myfile, $txt);
$txt="$" . "bodytext = " . "'#" . $bodytext . "';" . "\n";
fwrite ($myfile, $txt);
$txt="$" . "linkcolour = " . "'#" . $linkcolour . "';" . "\n";
fwrite ($myfile, $txt);
$txt="$" . "hlinkcolour = " . "'#" . $hlinkcolour . "';" . "\n";
fwrite ($myfile, $txt);
$txt="$" . "vlinkcolour = " . "'#" . $vlinkcolour . "';" . "\n";
fwrite ($myfile, $txt);
$txt="$" . "topbarbackgroundcolour = " . "'#" .
$topbarbackgroundcolour . "';" . "\n";
fwrite ($myfile, $txt);
$txt="$" . "topbartextcolour = " . "'#" . $topbartextcolour . "';" .
"\n";
fwrite ($myfile, $txt);
// callout panels
$txt="$" . "calloutbgcolour = " . "'#" . $calloutbgcolour . "';" .
"\n";
fwrite ($myfile, $txt);
$txt="$" . "calloutborder = " . "'#" . $calloutborder . "';" . "\n";
fwrite ($myfile, $txt);
$txt="$" . "callouttext = " . "'#" . $callouttext . "';" . "\n";
fwrite ($myfile, $txt);
//--------------------
$txt="$" . "calloutbgcolourp = " . "'#" . $calloutbgcolourp . "';" .
"\n";
fwrite ($myfile, $txt);
$txt="$" . "calloutborderp = " . "'#" . $calloutborderp . "';" .
"\n";
fwrite ($myfile, $txt);
$txt="$" . "callouttextp = " . "'#" . $callouttextp . "';" . "\n";
fwrite ($myfile, $txt);
```

—

```
//-------------------
$txt="$" . "calloutbgcolours = " . "'#" . $calloutbgcolours . "';" .
"\n";
fwrite ($myfile, $txt);
$txt="$" . "calloutborders = " . "'#" . $calloutborders . "';" .
"\n";
fwrite ($myfile, $txt);
$txt="$" . "callouttexts = " . "'#" . $callouttexts . "';" . "\n";
fwrite ($myfile, $txt);
//--------------------------
$txt="$" . "calloutbgcoloura = " . "'#" . $calloutbgcoloura . "';" .
"\n";
fwrite ($myfile, $txt);
$txt="$" . "calloutbordera = " . "'#" . $calloutbordera . "';" .
"\n";
fwrite ($myfile, $txt);
$txt="$" . "callouttexta = " . "'#" . $callouttexta . "';" . "\n";
fwrite ($myfile, $txt);
//------------------
$txt="$" . "calloutbgcolourss = " . "'#" . $calloutbgcolourss .
"';" . "\n";
fwrite ($myfile, $txt);
$txt="$" . "calloutborderss = " . "'#" . $calloutborderss . "';" .
"\n";
fwrite ($myfile, $txt);
$txt="$" . "callouttextss = " . "'#" . $callouttextss . "';" . "\n";
fwrite ($myfile, $txt);

//------------------------------------------
$txt="?" . ">" . "\n";
fwrite ($myfile, $txt);
fclose($myfile);
}
```

Once again I have to reiterate, this is just a small part of the actual program and does not include all the other parts necessary to make a fully functioning colour setter.

In the css code you will have to switch it over from.css to .php to use the colour values.

```php
<?


?>
<style type="text/css">
body {
  margin: 0;
  padding: 0;
  background: <?=$bodycolour?>;
  font-family: "Helvetica Neue", Helvetica, Roboto, Arial, sans-serif;
  font-weight: normal;
  line-height: 1.5;
  color: <?=$bodytext?>;
  -webkit-font-smoothing: antialiased;
  -moz-osx-font-smoothing: grayscale; }
  ...
  ...
  ...
  </style>
  <?


?>
```

Course you can leave the PHP CSS file as is or there are methods to convert it back into a pure CSSfile with you colour changes embedded.

Something Like this.

```php
<?
function ob_file_callback($buffer)
{
  global $ob_file;
```

—

```php
    fwrite($ob_file,$buffer);
}

// get file name
//$f=$_GET['f'];
//$f2=substr($f, 0 , (strrpos($f, ".")));
$f3="testall.css";
$ob_file = fopen($f3,'w');

ob_start('ob_file_callback');
include('../colours.php');

include ('maincssfile.php');
  include('ITSsitecolours.php');
 include('ITSbutton.php');
 include('ITStable.php');
   include('ITSaccordion.php');
   include('ITSforms.php');
  include('ITStabs.php');
    include('ITSswitch.php');
    include('ITStopbar.php');
    include('canvas.php');

    include('itsCard.php');

ob_end_flush();


//then we open it oup and remove style stuff
$newf=file_get_contents($f3);
$newf=str_replace('<style type="text/css">',"",$newf);
$newf=str_replace('</style>',"",$newf);
file_put_contents("ITScss.css",$newf);

echo " all Done ITScss.css created";

?>
```

—

Controlling User Input

In the early days of programming, everything had to fit into just a few kilobytes of memory so error control was minimal. For the most part, it was assumed that the user, would only input data that would be correct. Most computer users back then tended to be highly trained so mistakes were minimal but occasionally caused spectacular crashes and corrupt data.

Today, most users are functionally computer literate and thus input must be rigorously controlled. Everything from a simple email address to document uploads and more need to be scrutinized and corrective measures taken.

This is not nearly as daunting as it sounds however you as a programmer have to take all responsibility for the code, making sure that you're getting exactly what you asked for.

Consider something as simple as a login.

You're only asking for a couple of different things, perhaps a email address and a password. Often times most users simply copy and paste the information into whatever text boxes that you are using to gather the data. That often means that you have extra spaces mixed in with the text.

johndoe@someplace.com has an extra space in front of it and can cause problems when checking the details in the database.

You Must Login

Not a Member? click here to join

Email

[   ]

Password

[   ]

Login

The simple solution is to use the TRIM command to remove any leading or trailing spaces. Now as can be seen from the form above, we are asking for two pieces of information.

The user's email address and your password, that seems simple enough for the user to input the data we require.

Instead of their email address, they put their name. The password now is either typed wrong or copy and pasted with extra spaces so when they hit the button, the login fails.

Controlling the input is the programmers job. To make sure we get the data that we require, we have to insert error catching code and then send the form back to the user with hints for inputting the correct information.

—

So now instead of just doing this.

```php
if( isset ($_POST ['mypassword']) && isset($_POST ['useremail'])) {

$tpass = $_POST ['mypassword'];
$temail = $_POST ['useremail'];
// check info in database
}
```

WE have to check for errors and wrong data.

```php
if( isset ($_POST ['mypassword']) && isset($_POST ['useremail'])) {
//clear error values
$emailflag = 0;
$badflag = 0;
$badmail = "That is not an Email address";
// checking information


$tpass = $_POST ['mypassword'];
$tpass = trim ($tpass);
$temail = $_POST ['useremail'];
$temail = strtolower ($tuser);
$temail = trim ($temail);
// make sure it has the @ sign

if (filter_var($temail, FILTER_VALIDATE_EMAIL)) {
//email address is considered valid
}else{
//invalid email
$emailflag = 1;
$badflag++;
```

```
}

$_SESSION ['pass'] = $tpass;
$_SESSION['user'] = $temail;

if ($badflag == 0 {
// check info in database
// if correct send to another page ie members area etc

}else{

// send user back to form with errors

}
```

As you can see we've had to add more code to account for what may possibly be done wrong by the user but it doesn't end there.

There is also security to think about. Malicious hackers and bots can try to break in to your server, gain access to your database or other unwanted actions. You have to account for all that and take the necessary steps to stop it from happening. For more information see the chapter on security.

—

One of the other problems is that if you have a text area and the user is putting a couple of paragraphs of information what they're also using apostrophes single quotes and double quotes. This tends to generate an error when you trying to send that information to your database. There are many workarounds for this including addslashes() which adds a \, effectively becomes an escape for the apostrophe or quote. This also means when you retrieve the information for the database you have to reverse the process and remove the slashes using stripslashes(). Another way is to utilize str_replace () and change the apostrophe to under score _character. Once again you also have to reverse the process when your extract information in the database. Depending upon your data, is which method you should use or prefer to use because searching the database that contains entries with apostrophes and quotes can yield unpredictable results.

We created a database for spelling and chose to use the under score character to replace apostrophes because we knew for sure that there is no double quotes. This way we search for a word that contains an apostrophe we simply use str_replace to change the apostrophe to an _because that is how it is represented in the database.(ie can't can_t)

Most of user input will come from forms that you're having them fill out. Another type of user input does not use the $_POSTcommand, it uses the $_GET command which is similar but gets its data from the command line instead as well as a few other sources.

We've all seen on places like Facebook, when you click a link in the browser area that gives you the website name will also have a whole string of numbers and letters in all kinds of other information. This is considered to be the command line.

http://mywebsite.com/index.php?x=2&y=bob&syn=h54gh 64TYwer

Both POST and GET send back an array to be processed and that is why you'll see square back brackets being utilized. $_GET ['x'] , the x that you see represents itself as a string but it also is the key that allows you to access the value of x, in this case the number 2.

First we have to check to make sure that we have a variable to work with.
We use the ISSET command.

```
if ( isset ($_GET['x'] )){
// next because we know that x should be a number we check to
make sure that it is
  $x = $_GET['x'];

    if (is_numeric ($x))
    {
    // true $x is a number
    }else{
    // false $x is not a number. HMM there is a problem
    }
}
```

If X is not a number then it is possible that someone has altered the command line for whatever reason, possibly a hacking attempt. For the most part, you the programmer are setting the command line parameters and should not be changed by the user for any reason.

All of the command line should be checked for data that is consistent with what it's supposed to be. In the case of Y, the return value should be Bob

```
$string = 'bob{[)($8&!';
if (ctype_alpha($string)) {
echo "The string consists of all letters.<br>";
} else {
```

—

```
echo "The string does not consist of all letters.<br>";
}
```

When we run the test to make sure that it only contains alpha characters and what that means is rechecking to make sure that they are all just letters, if we find an alteration we can act upon it.

The above example will tell you that the string does not consist of all letters. However if the Y key has not been altered it will return true because the value is set to bob.

That particular routine is case insensitive as well.

No matter how time-consuming the coding can be you must test everything from the user and the command line or your results at best will be unpredictable and at worst you will get hacked.

It is up to you as a web developer and/or programmer to control every aspect of a website including whatever uses of that website will throw at you. A lot of times it is not a deliberate effort to circumvent or hack the website, it's usually just users not knowing what they're doing. It is up to you to account for that and provide a seamless interaction between the users and the website.

Security

There are many aspects to deal with security and all of them are important.

Whether you trying to secure your server, website or admin menus, there are various aspects that need to be dealt with.

WordPress is a very popular website development tool in many website designers opt for it. WordPress itself was a very well written PHP project however the main failing is security. The people who develop WordPress constantly update it trying to stay ahead of security flaws and problems. This is not enough because the code for WordPress is freely available and that means hackers can and will sift through the entire collection of PHP scripts looking for vulnerabilities. Next we have problems with plug-ins that have the same security concern because once again the code is available and readable by anyone.

In a typical WordPress installation, the main program as well as plug-ins and themes are installed. Any one of these can become a weak link in the security chain. WordPress websites are the most hacked in the world. True if set up correctly with as much security as possible, it does limit but doesn't completely mitigate the security risks.

As a website designer and PHP programmer, it is up to you to ensure the security of your code, website and database.

One of the main aspects of PHP is that it is virtually impossible without using FTP or something similar, to view the actual PHP code. Your code will never be seen by anyone without the proper or control. Now that doesn't mean it can't be hacked, just that now is much more difficult.

—

Email access from forms needs to be controlled so that you don't become deluged with spam. Passwords stored in the database need to be encrypted or otherwise secured in a different manner. The code itself, that you write needs to be rigorously tested for security flaws. On the server itself, if you have direct access or control, these all security patches updated as quickly as possible.

For servers, most are running a UNIX variant of some sort, generally CentOS or Red Hat being some of the most popular. Most server providers will also include cPanel as part of your server. They may or may not charge a fee for this however paying the fee is worthwhile.

Brute force access is the most commonly used hacking tool. They will keep trying password after password until finally they get it right and at that point, they are in and can do whatever they want.

cPHulk is one of the security tools available in cPanel, more correctly in the WHM part of cPanel. It is relatively easy to use, contains a white list and a blacklist as well as settings that determine how many times someone can try to login to anything server related before they're locked out. The lockout is temporary but can last a few weeks. To make it permanent, you simply add the IP address to the blacklist. On our servers, we have the values set very low. To login attempts maximum and then you're locked out. We also have an extensive blacklist in use that locks out vast majority of the world. Bear in mind this, this only applies server related access. SSH, FTP, email SMTP(sending) as well as a few other things but it does not impact whether or not the website is visible to these people. They can be locked out and still see the website unless you taken extra measures to ensure they get to see nothing.

An example of that is that your website maintains its own white list and blacklist in IP addresses are added as needed for whatever reason. If you determine that someone is attempting to hack your website than adding them to the blacklist will indeed stop all access to the website for the and you can choose to show them nothing is in a blank page or a page that informs him that all the details have been logged etc.

Either way you are controlling access. There are ways to lock out entire countries from being able to access your website.

—

Harden Your PHP for Better Security

There are ways to make your PHP more resistant to attacks. Considered to be hardening your PHP and is available by setting various values in your PHP.ini file. If you've access and are allowed to make changes to that file then you may want to consider some of the options laid out below.

You will need to open the file in an editor or on cPanel this can be done directly from the menu and you choose advanced options.

Remote settings:

Is advisable to not allow fopen wrappers to open remote URLs. Remote content is not necessarily trustworthy and therefore disabling the option means that fopen will only work with local content. In the event that you absolutely require fopen to work remotely then do not change the setting.

```
allow_url_fopen = 0
allow_url_include = 0
```

As well it is usually unadvisable to use include files that are remote however sometimes it is necessary.

Runtime Settings:

In the scope of things you want to be able to limit how much time is allowed for input as well as the time that a script can run. In case a script becomes compromised we will not read more input or run excessively consuming massive resources in the process.

```
max_input_time = 30
```

max_execution_time = 30

Setting both of these values to 30 is recommended mainly because most well written. PHP scripts do not require running for longer than that although there are exceptions. This is generally when you're passing to an internal server routine or program that is using a large quantity of data.

Memory Limits:

Ensure that a PHP script never utilizes more than 8MB of memory. In case a script was compromised, this setting effectively limits the amount of memory that the script can utilize.

memory_limit = 8M

Register Globals:

This was utilized in PHP three and four but by default now it is switched off because it represents a huge security risk. It is advisable to leave this off because most modern scripts will not utilize it anyways and shouldn't.

register_globals = off

Expose PHP:

The presence of PHP as well as version numbers are exposed as part of HTTP responses and this allows unnecessary insight into the server which is not required. It is advisable to turn it off.

expose_php = 0

Force Redirect:

—

This ensures that PHP can only be run through Web server redirect rules and prevents of being called directly which definitely improves security.

cgi.force_redirect = 1

Input Data Restrictions:

Limiting post size as well as the maximum input variables allowed effectively helps when hackers try to flood web applications with large amounts of data. This will slow down server response and may crash the server. This can also impact the file size that can be uploaded so it is essential that you make them match.

post_max_size = 256K
max_input_vars = 100
upload_max_filesize = 256K

Error Messages:

Error messages only be displayed during testing phases and never available to the user. Error codes can contain detailed information about the code and the server and can be potentially utilized by hackers. You can still log errors that you can go over at a later date.

log_errors = 1
error_log = /home/mywebsite/error_log // _mywebsite should be replaced by the actual name_

Open basedir Tweak:

Setting this variable directly is easily available but you must also include any and all paths required. CPanel offers this as a security tweak and will set it up automatically and correctly. This ensures that only files in the list of directories are accessible and prevents PHP scripts from accidentally or otherwise using files outside of the white list paths.

```
open_basedir = "/home/username/public_html"
or
open_basedir =
"/home/username/public_html:/var/lib/php/tmp_upload:
/var/lib/php/session"
```

File Uploads:

If your website does not utilize file uploads then you should set this value to zero. This will prevent hackers from even attempting to upload malicious scripts.

```
file_uploads = 0
```
Now if it is a requirement that users are allowed to upload files then you have to set this value to one but you can also restrict the size of the file. Bearing in mind it has to be lower than or equal to post_max_size. Please note that none of these values restrict in any way what you can upload by FTP.

```
file_uploads = 1
upload_max_filesize = 1M
```

Session Security:

You need to set a new session ID if the browser has sent an uninitialized ID this prevents session fixation attacks. As well you should set .sessions to strict mode as this reduces the risk of session interception.

—

```
session.use_strict_mode = 1
session.cookie_httponly = 1
```

Next we want to save the session ID in a cookie rather than a get parameter or post parameter

```
session.name = custom_session_id
```

We want the session cookie to be accessible only from an HTTP request and not other sources like JavaScript because it prevents XSS attacks.
```
session.use_cookies = 1
session.use_only_cookies = 1
session.use_trans_sid = 0
```

Check where the request came from in order to determine whether to allow access to session data. Update this setting value to your application's domain name to help prevent session information from being accessed if a script is loaded from an external source.

```
session.referer_check = yourwebsite.com
```

Website Security:

PHP has many functions and commands that can be used however some present more of a security risk than others in the simplest solution is to not allow them to run in the first place. In your PHP INI file you can selectively disable any function that you are not going to use without impacting the usability of PHP.

CPanel updates can also cause some confusion because certain functions like EXEC and SYSTEM can be turned off by default and are not easy to turn back on. If you require the use these functions then you need to make sure that when you're updating Apache and PHP that these functions are not automatically configured as not allowed. As well cPanel now allows you to run multiple versions of PHP so it is up to you to make sure that your code applies to the version that you want to use.

Disable Vulnerable Functions
disable_functions =
ini_set,php_uname,getmyuid,getmypid,passthru,leak,listen,diskfreespace,tmpfile,link,ignore_user_abord,shell_exec,dl,set_time_limit,exec,system,highlight_file,source,show_source,fpaththru,virtual,posix_ctermid,posix_getcwd,posix_getegid,posix_geteuid,posix_getgid,posix_getgrgid,posix_getgrnam,posix_getgroups,posix_getlogin,posix_getpgid,posix_getpgrp,posix_getpid,posix,_getppid,posix_getpwnam,posix_getpwuid,posix_getrlimit,posix_getsid,posix_getuid,posix_isatty,posix_kill,posix_mkfifo,posix_setegid,posix_seteuid,posix_setgid,posix_setpgid,posix_setsid,posix_setuid,posix_times,posix_ttyname,posix_uname,proc_open,proc_close,proc_get_status,proc_nice,proc_terminate,phpinfo,popen,curl_exec,curl_multi_exec,parse_ini_file,allow_url_fopen,allow_url_include,pcntl_exec,chgrp,chmod,chown,lchgrp,lchown,putenv

—

Directories

One of the most common problems are known directories. In WordPress and other CRM's all directories and structures for those directories are known as well as various login aspects.

We create a lot of auto installing PHP code. The challenge becomes making the directories less predictable. This can be done in a variety of different ways.

Using code similar to the below, we can easily create a random directory name that will not be easy to guess. We pass it two parameters, the length of the directory name and whatever characters we wanted to start with.

```php
// __ _ Random Directory Name __ __ _
function ITcreateDir($length,$startcharacters) {
$chars = "AabBCdeFfGhjkKmMNnpQRstTuZzvwXy23456789";

$i = 0;
$newdirectoryname = $startcharacters ;
   while ($i <= $length) {
      $num = rand() % 33;
      $tmp = substr($chars, $num, 1);
      $newdirectoryname = $newdirectoryname . $tmp;
      $i++;
   }
return $newdirectoryname;
}


$mynewDirectoryName= ITcreateDir(30,'Km');
```

This particular technique can be utilized for more than just directory names, you can also be used for renaming files as part of an automated install. Some directories that you may want to hide our admin directories, downloadable files locations and others.

If your server set up correctly then it should not allow access to the directory structure. What we mean by that is that Apache and others follow a set of rules that if a default file is not found then it can instead display the directory list. Under no circumstances should you allow this to happen.

The robots.txt file that sits in the root directory will only tell compliant search bots what directories they can and cannot search through. It does not allow any access to the actual directory structure and the search bot has no way to gain that information.

Logins

If your website utilizes logins for users to access various areas of the website, it is not enough just to have them login. Every webpage on your site must somehow reflect whether or not they are logged in and information is allowed to be shown. This is generally done through cookies and sessions.

```
session_start();
// switch to secure mode HTTPS
if ( ! isset ($_SERVER['HTTPS'])) {
header('Location: https://' . $_SERVER["SERVER_NAME"] .
$_SERVER['REQUEST_URI']);
}
if (isset($_COOKIE ["userid"])){
$cookieOK = $_COOKIE ["userid"];
$_SESSION ['userLogin'] = 1;
$_SESSION ['userid'] = $cookieOK;
$UserID = $_SESSION['userid'];
$cookieSet="Yes";
$userLogin = 1;
}else{
$userLogin = 0;
$cookieSet = "No";
```

—

```
//$pt=0;
}
if (isset ($_SESSION['userid'])){
$UserID = $_SESSION['userid'];
}else{
$UserID ="";
}

if ($userLogin==1){
// User is Logged in display member page
 include ('memberpage.php');

}else{
// user is NOT Logged in display regular page
 include ('nonmemberpage.php');
}
```

There are numerous other things you can do to secure logins. You can use the IP address to check the country. You can use the session ID against what you have stored in a database. When asking users for details for logins are they compliant with what you're asking. Often times to check whether or not a hacker is attempting to gain access by simply looking for things that shouldn't be there. A lot of logins ask for an email address as part of the information required. If this does not conform to an email address and contains extra characters an apostrophe, brackets, parenthesis or something similar, it is more likely hacking attempt and should be dealt with immediately as it is not likely simply user error.

Session IDs are supposed to be absolutely unique, and most of the time they are however there's a couple of caveats involved. The session ID is generated but is also unique to the device. What that means is that if you go to your website on your phone, the session ID will stay the same even if you go back a month later. Most of the information available through Google search about session IDs says that should not happen and that the session ID is regenerated uniquely each time. We have found that is not the case and the actual session IDs are quite durable. It is not just the IP address that is being utilized to generate the session ID, because if you login on your computer as opposed to your phone, each will produce a different session ID even though your IP address remains the same. This particular information can also be utilized to further secure logins.

—

Database Security:

Database security is an often overlooked aspect when considering the security of your code and your website. All login passwords should not be stored as plain text, they should be stored either **as a hash** or encrypted in some other manner. Storing them as a hash value is probably the easiest and most reliable as long as you follow a few simple rules, they should also be unbreakable. Using two salt values and the password will likely yield an extremely unique hash value and one that is difficult to replicate.

Whatever using for salt values should not be stored in the database, they should be stored in a simple text file with the unique name that would not be easy to guess.

Some sites store credit card details and these are the most at risk. If a hacker somehow gains access to your database, these details could be stolen. Your website must use the HTTPS protocol as this encrypts information sent to and from the server. Any information in the database for credit cards must also utilize serious encryption. Unless you absolutely have to have credit card details for your website is far better off as a third party service to process credit card transactions.

Whatever using for salt values should not be stored in the database, they should be stored in a simple text file with the unique name that would not be easy to guess or can be stored in PHP file as variables.

Making backups of your database on a regular basis is also recommended. Anything can happen, your server may crash or hard drive failure, backups allow you to put the information back in whereas it may not be absolutely complete, it is better than starting from scratch.

One of the best practices for database security is limited access. Under no circumstances should users of the website be allowed in any form access to the database. Only people that need access to the database should be allowed access. This should be as few people as possible.

—

Building Websites

The most common use of PHP is building dynamic websites that allow different information to be displayed dependent upon circumstances.

Entire pages can be stored in a database or file and then presented easily to the end user. Full back ends for administration are also possible that would not be available as a static webpage.

The very first thing you have to know about web pages is that almost everything is stored as a text file or a database entry. PHP allows you to make modifications and adjust parameters to display only what you want, when you want.

In HTML, tags are used to inform the browser of one of webpages supposed to look like. An example is font colours and font sizes. There are also division tags and a wealth of others that help control the final look of a webpage. PHP pre-processes all of the code before it is sent to the browser as HTML.

There are very simple ways to ensure that every webpage that you display has a consistent look and feel to it. Most websites are no less than five pages but could extend into hundreds of pages.

Without PHP, every single page would have to be coded individually. It is far simpler and easier to create a template that will ensure that all the pages have the same look and layout.

```
<?

include('preheader.php');

?>
<title> <?=$sitename?> | <?=$pagename?> </title>
```

```
<?
include ('header.php');

$filelocation= $themedir."indexmain.php";

include ($filelocation);

include ('footer.php');
?>
```

This represents a very simple template that uses a pre-header, header, a content page and the footer to display an entire webpage. As you can see the template file is actually quite small because it is calling in pages that are filled with more code.

This particular technique allows you to simplify the process while maintaining consistency throughout the entire website.

The pre-header contains the code that may include session and session variables as well as configuration routines for the database.

The header will probably contain the basics of the HTML including all the CSS and possibly some JavaScript that needs to run first.

We use file location to include the file that is relevant to this particular page.

The footer are likely to contain the rest of the JavaScript and whatever finalizations are needed for the HTML.

One of the most important things to remember is that path to files are relative to the original calling file. What that means is that the path is determined by the calling file so in our case we are using a variable called $themedir which represents the directory relative to the original file.

—

In this case it will be our index file index.php. What makes it important is that if any the other files are including files you have to make sure that the path that they are using is correct relative to the original calling file.

If *indexmain.php* uses any include statements, they must be pathed from the original index file and not in relation to their particular location from the second file.

colours.php is located in off the root directory in a directory called extra

include ('extra/colours.php'); // is correct

include ('../extra/colours.php'); // is incorrect

Another solution for pathing issues is to use the absolute path which would look something like this.

include ('home/mywebsite/public_html/extra/colours.php')

By using templates to simplify the process of building the entire website. Every aspect that is reusable can be included as a separate file. That means menus and page layouts will need to be written once and then included to become part of the current page. Menus themselves if stored in a separate file can be easily changed with items added or deleted and thus affect the entire website without having to go through dozens of pages making changes.

We use templates and code that we written as a basis for all websites we develop whether they be e-commerce or simple information pages.

This massively cuts down on programming time and development costs.

WordPress has extensive admin areas for making instantaneous changes to website. You can follow the same idea and whether or not it is you making the changes or your customer, a well-designed admin area makes life very easy.

Entire pages of information can be stored in a database making them easy to change. You can use TinyMCE which is similar to a word processor in a text area to add make changes to various areas of the website in the admin menu.

NOTE:

Any time there is the ability to make profound changes to a website you must absolutely protect and provide the security necessary to only allow those authorized to make the changes.

There are many tools already available for you to use while designing your website. There are tons of JavaScript code available, CSS frameworks (foundation , bootstrap and others) as well as JavaScript frameworks like Jquery and many more. There are also PHP frameworks that you can use, like Zend, Cakewalk and others. All of these will simplify and help reduce development time.

For e-commerce once again there are a ton of options in prewritten shopping carts that can be easily added to any website or you can get adventurous and write your own, which is not as difficult as it sounds.

There is a wealth of tools already at your disposal that you can take advantage of you don't have to reinvent the wheel. Searching the Internet can produce quantities of code, examples as well as prewritten classes and frameworks that will allow you website to have all the necessary bling.

—

AJAX

Ajax gives your website the ability to make display changes various information without resorting to a page refresh.

Asynchronous JavaScript And XML

First off the AJAX is not a programming language or by itself a tool. It runs client-side and allows it to communicate to and from the server without needing to post back or need a complete page refresh.

Ajax is a generic term for JavaScript techniques used to connect to Web servers dynamically and usually uses XmlHttpRequest objects to interact with the Web server dynamically via JavaScript.

In essence there are various parts to Ajax that are utilized, most commonly, JavaScript, PHP and JSon.

A simple explanation of how to accomplish this, a user presses a button on the website which is been hooked to a JavaScript function. The JavaScript function then sends a XmlHttpRequest generally as post to a PHP page. Once the return of the PHP pages complete the XmlHttpRequest updates whatever section of the web site you have chosen.

Example you would include this as javacript js file directly in the HTML.

```
<script src="js/myajax.js"></script>
```

And the button code

```
<input id="bt<?=$tid?>" class ="small button round"
type="submit" name="Submit" value =" Send This"
onclick="ajaxRequestB('send','tv<?=$tid?>','bt<?=$tid?>','<?=$t
id?>');">
```

Would be embedded in the page that you want to use it on.

```
//Ajax Request Handler
function xmlhttpPost (url, method, divname, ht, qstr){
__ var xmlHttpReq = false;
__ var self = this;

__ document.getElementById (divname).innerHTML = "<div
class= 'panel3 radius3' ><br><center><img src= 'ajax-loader.gif'
/> </center> </div>";

__ // Mozilla/Safari
__ __ if (window.XMLHttpRequest){
__ __ self.xmlHttpReq = new XMLHttpRequest();
__ __ }
__ // IE
__ __ else if (window.ActiveXObject){
__ __ self.xmlHttpReq = new
ActiveXObject('Microsoft.XMLHTTP');
__ __ }
__ self.xmlHttpReq.open (method, url, true);
__ self.xmlHttpReq.setRequestHeader ('Content-Type',
'application/x-www-form-urlencoded');
__ self.xmlHttpReq.onreadystatechange = function(){
__ __ if (self.xmlHttpReq.readyState == 4){

__ __ updateDiv (self.xmlHttpReq.responseText ,divname,
ht);//div update function call

__ __ }
__ }
```

—

```
__ self.xmlHttpReq.send (qstr);
}


//Updating output
function updateDiv (txtvalue, divname, ht){
   __ if (divname){
   __ document.getElementById (divname).innerHTML='';
   __ document.getElementById (divname).innerHTML=txtvalue;
   __ document.getElementById (ht).focus();
   __//document.getElementById (target).focus();
   __}
}
function ajaxRequestB (process, divname ,ht, uid){

   __ if(process =='send'){
   __
   __ qstr    = 'p=' + escape(process) + '&uid=' + uid ;
   __ xmlhttpPos t('ajaxSend.php' ,'POST', divname, ht, qstr);

   __
   __}
   __
}__
```

Ajax is great at updating webpages dynamically however tracking down errors can be a nightmare. The PHP page that you send the information to be processed can have an error that doesn't show up. The JavaScript itself can produce an error and even in the Web console of the browser not give you any real explanation for the error that is helpful.

All Ajax must be tested under a variety of different conditions to make sure that is working correctly and producing the expected results.

Once you get the hang of using Ajax it will be a very useful tool in your arsenal.

The above is just a very simplified version of manually setting up your own Ajax response JQuery, Zepto , Prototype and others have built-in routines specifically for dealing with Ajax.

—

Error Control

Errors are quite common in any programming language and trick of course is to catch them before they spiral out of control.

Debug:

all your code these to have debug routines to make it easier to track down errors but he should never be shown to the end user.

```
<?
$debug=1;
if ($debug==1){

ini_set('display_errors', 1);
ini_set('display_startup_errors', 1);
error_reporting(E_ALL);

}
?>
```

However, this doesn't make PHP to show parse errors - the only way to show those errors is to modify your php.ini with this line:

display_errors = on

This represents the simplest way to find or this problem for the code. Not just syntax errors but various functions can become depreciated and not likely to work in future versions of PHP that may be upgraded on the server. Pay attention to all the error messages you get why you're debugging.

Exception:

PHP 5 came a new object oriented way of dealing with errors.

Exception handling is used to change the normal flow of the code execution if a specified error (exceptional) condition occurs.
This condition is called an exception.

This is what usually happens when an exception is triggered:

The current code state is saved
The code execution will switch to a predefined (custom) exception handler function
Depending on the situation, the handler may then resume the execution from the saved code state,
terminate the script execution or continue the script from a different location in the code

```
//create function with an exception
function checkValue($number) {
  if($number>1) {
    throw new Exception("Value must be 1 or below");
  }
  return true;
}
checkValue(4);
```

—

Fatal error: Uncaught exception 'Exception' with message
'Value must be 1 or below' in
/home/someaccount/public_html/fbook/echeck.php:5 Stack
trace: #0
/home/someaccount/public_html/fbook/echeck.php(9):
checkValue(4) #1 {main} thrown in
/home/someaccount/public_html/fbook/echeck.php on line
5

As you can see this produces an error mainly because the
exception has nowhere to go and is not being called properly.
You have to use the TRY command
    PHP error handling keywords

The following keywords are used for PHP exception
handling.

    Try: The try block contains the code that may potentially
throw an exception. All of the code within the try block is
executed until an exception is potentially thrown.
    Throw: The throw keyword is used to signal the
occurrence of a PHP exception. The PHP runtime will then try
to find a catch statement to handle the exception.
    Catch: This block of code will be called only if an
exception occurs within the try code block. The code within
your catch statement must handle the exception that was
thrown.
    Finally: In PHP 5.5, the finally statement is introduced.
The finally block may also be specified after or instead of catch
blocks. Code within the finally block will always be executed
after the try and catch blocks, regardless of whether an
exception has been thrown, and before normal execution
resumes.
    This is useful for scenarios like closing a database
connection or files regardless if an exception occurred or not.

```php
try {
    // run your code here
}
catch (exception $e) {
    //code to handle the exception
}
finally {
    //optional code that always runs
}

//create function with an exception
function checkValue($number) {
  if($number>1) {
    throw new Exception("Value must be 1 or below");
  }
  return true;
}

//trigger exception in a "try" block
$myvalue=5;
try {
$test= checkValue($myvalue);
  //If the exception is thrown, this text will not be shown
  echo 'MyValue is a number with a value of 1 or below<br>';
  echo " Value of Test $test which means it is TRUE<br>";
}

//catch exception
catch(Exception $e) {
  echo 'Message: ' .$e->getMessage();
}
```

Result:

Message: Value must be 1 or below

—

There is also a simpler PHP version of error control utilizing various functions and commands.

is_numeric checks to see if a value is a number or not and you can branch accordingly.

```
if (is_numeric($myvalue))
{
echo "$myvalue is Numeric.<br>" ;
}else{
echo "$myvalue is not Numeric. <br>" ;
// or we can send it back to the user in a different way
$ecode=1;
$ecode="Numbers Only";
}
```

Then simply display the error back to the user in the appropriate area.

There are a variety of different commands you can use a check input including isset.

END STUFF

Some have suggested that PHP is now a dying language soon to be replaced by other programming languages such as Python. Python itself is an excellent programming language and can do many things that PHP can also do. The main problem is that Python runs at server level similar to how PHP runs at server level.

Server level is also all about security. Python has to be called explicitly and unlike PHP, does not have the correct permissions to be able to be allowed to run on a highly secure environment. System calls in a lot of servers are heavily restricted. On most shared hosting, which the vast majority of regular website utilize, do not allow system-level calls. Because PHP is built into the system it is allowed to run whereas Python may not.

PHP is constantly being improved and updated and there is no reason to believe that level of commitment from the programmers that control PHP are going to stop.

This makes it a worthwhile effort on your part to continue to use and improve your PHP code.

—

Mysql Data Types

TEXT TYPES
CHAR( ) __ A fixed section from 0 to 255 characters long.
VARCHAR( ) __ A variable section from 0 to 255 characters long.
TINYTEXT __ A string with a maximum length of 255 characters.
TEXT __ A string with a maximum length of 65535 characters.
BLOB __ A string with a maximum length of 65535 characters.
MEDIUMTEXT __ A string with a maximum length of 16777215 characters.
MEDIUMBLOB __ A string with a maximum length of 16777215 characters.
LONGTEXT __ A string with a maximum length of 4294967295 characters.
LONGBLOB __ A string with a maximum length of 4294967295 characters.

The ( ) brackets allow you to enter a maximum number of characters will be used in the column.
VARCHAR(20)
CHAR and VARCHAR are the most widely used types. CHAR is a fixed length string and is mainly used when the data is not going to vary much in it's length. VARCHAR is a variable length string and is mainly used when the data may vary in length.

CHAR may be faster for the database to process considering the fields stay the same length down the column. VARCHAR may be a bit slower as it calculates each field down the column, but it saves on memory space. Which one to ultimatly use is up to you.

Using both a CHAR and VARCHAR option in the same table, MySQL will automatically change the CHAR into VARCHAR for compatability reasons.

BLOB stands for Binary Large OBject. Both TEXT and BLOB are variable length types that store large amounts of data. They are similar to a larger version of VARCHAR. These types can store a large piece of data information, but they are also processed much slower.

NUMBER TYPES

TINYINT( ) __ -128 to 127 normal
0 to 255 UNSIGNED.

SMALLINT( ) __ -32768 to 32767 normal
0 to 65535 UNSIGNED.

MEDIUMINT( ) __ -8388608 to 8388607 normal
0 to 16777215 UNSIGNED.

INT( ) __ -2147483648 to 2147483647 normal
0 to 4294967295 UNSIGNED.

BIGINT( ) __ -9223372036854775808 to 9223372036854775807 normal
0 to 18446744073709551615 UNSIGNED.

FLOAT __ A small number with a floating decimal point.

DOUBLE(,) __ A large number with a floating decimal point.

DECIMAL(,) __ A DOUBLE stored as a string , allowing for a fixed decimal point.

—

The integer types have an extra option called UNSIGNED. Normally, the integer goes from a negative to positive value. Using an UNSIGNED command will move that range up so it starts at zero instead of a negative number.

DATE TYPES

DATE   YYYY-MM-DD.

MISC TYPES

ENUM ( ) __ Short for ENUMERATION which means that each column may have one of a specified possible values.

SET __ Similar to ENUM except each column may have more than one of the specified possible values.

ENUM is short for ENUMERATED list. This column can only store one of the values that are declared in the specified list contained in the ( ) brackets.

ENUM('y','n')

You can list up to 65535 values in an ENUM list. If a value is inserted that is not in the list, a blank value will be inserted.

SET is similar to ENUM except SET may contain up to 64 list items and can store more than one choice.

MYSQL Keywords and Reserved Words

ACCESSIBLE, Reserved
ACCOUNT, Keyword, added in 5.7
ACTION, Keyword
ADD, Reserved
ADMIN, Reserved, added in 8.0
AFTER, Keyword
AGAINST, Keyword
AGGREGATE, Keyword
ALGORITHM, Keyword
ALL, Reserved
ALTER, Reserved
ALWAYS, Keyword, added in 5.7
ANALYSE, Keyword, added in 5.6.6; removed in 8.0
ANALYZE, Reserved
AND, Reserved
ANY, Keyword
AS, Reserved
ASC, Reserved
ASCII, Keyword
ASENSITIVE, Reserved
AT, Keyword
AUTHORS, Keyword, removed in 5.6.8
AUTOEXTEND_SIZE, Keyword
AUTO_INCREMENT, Keyword
AVG, Keyword
AVG_ROW_LENGTH, Keyword
BACKUP, Keyword
BEFORE, Reserved
BEGIN, Keyword
BETWEEN, Reserved
BIGINT, Reserved
BINARY, Reserved
BINLOG, Keyword
BIT, Keyword
BLOB, Reserved
BLOCK, Keyword
BOOL, Keyword
BOOLEAN, Keyword
BOTH, Reserved
BTREE, Keyword
BUCKETS, Keyword, added in 8.0
BY, Reserved
BYTE, Keyword
CACHE, Keyword
CALL, Reserved

CASCADE, Reserved
CASCADED, Keyword
CASE, Reserved
CATALOG_NAME, Keyword
CHAIN, Keyword
CHANGE, Reserved
CHANGED, Keyword
CHANNEL, Keyword, added in 5.7
CHAR, Reserved
CHARACTER, Reserved
CHARSET, Keyword
CHECK, Reserved
CHECKSUM, Keyword
CIPHER, Keyword
CLASS_ORIGIN, Keyword
CLIENT, Keyword
CLONE, Keyword, added in 8.0
CLOSE, Keyword
COALESCE, Keyword
CODE, Keyword
COLLATE, Reserved
COLLATION, Keyword
COLUMN, Reserved
COLUMNS, Keyword
COLUMN_FORMAT, Keyword, added in 5.6.6
COLUMN_NAME, Keyword
COMMENT, Keyword
COMMIT, Keyword
COMMITTED, Keyword
COMPACT, Keyword
COMPLETION, Keyword
COMPONENT, Keyword, added in 8.0
COMPRESSED, Keyword
COMPRESSION, Keyword, added in 5.7
CONCURRENT, Keyword
CONDITION, Reserved
CONNECTION, Keyword
CONSISTENT, Keyword
CONSTRAINT, Reserved
CONSTRAINT_CATALOG, Keyword
CONSTRAINT_NAME, Keyword
CONSTRAINT_SCHEMA, Keyword
CONTAINS, Keyword
CONTEXT, Keyword
CONTINUE, Reserved
CONTRIBUTORS, Keyword, removed in 5.6.8
CONVERT, Reserved
CPU, Keyword

CREATE, Reserved
CROSS, Reserved
CUBE, Keyword
CUME_DIST, Reserved, added in 8.0
CURRENT, Keyword, added in 5.6.4
CURRENT_DATE, Reserved
CURRENT_TIME, Reserved
CURRENT_TIMESTAMP, Reserved
CURRENT_USER, Reserved
CURSOR, Reserved
CURSOR_NAME, Keyword
DATA, Keyword
DATABASE, Reserved
DATABASES, Reserved
DATAFILE, Keyword
DATE, Keyword
DATETIME, Keyword
DAY, Keyword
DAY_HOUR, Reserved
DAY_MICROSECOND, Reserved
DAY_MINUTE, Reserved
DAY_SECOND, Reserved
DEALLOCATE, Keyword
DEC, Reserved
DECIMAL, Reserved
DECLARE, Reserved
DEFAULT, Reserved
DEFAULT_AUTH, Keyword, added in 5.6.4
DEFINER, Keyword
DEFINITION, Keyword, added in 8.0
DELAYED, Reserved
DELAY_KEY_WRITE, Keyword
DELETE, Reserved
DENSE_RANK, Reserved, added in 8.0
DESC, Reserved
DESCRIBE, Reserved
DESCRIPTION, Keyword, added in 8.0
DES_KEY_FILE, Keyword, removed in 8.0
DETERMINISTIC, Reserved
DIAGNOSTICS, Keyword, added in 5.6.4
DIRECTORY, Keyword
DISABLE, Keyword
DISCARD, Keyword
DISK, Keyword
DISTINCT, Reserved
DISTINCTROW, Reserved
DIV, Reserved
DO, Keyword

—

DOUBLE, Reserved
DROP, Reserved
DUAL, Reserved
DUMPFILE, Keyword
DUPLICATE, Keyword
DYNAMIC, Keyword
EACH, Reserved
ELSE, Reserved
ELSEIF, Reserved
EMPTY, Reserved, added in 8.0
ENABLE, Keyword
ENCLOSED, Reserved
ENCRYPTION, Keyword, added in 5.7
END, Keyword
ENDS, Keyword
ENGINE, Keyword
ENGINES, Keyword
ENUM, Keyword
ERROR, Keyword, added in 5.5.3
ERRORS, Keyword
ESCAPE, Keyword
ESCAPED, Reserved
EVENT, Keyword
EVENTS, Keyword
EVERY, Keyword
EXCEPT, Reserved, added in 8.0
EXCHANGE, Keyword
EXCLUDE, Keyword, added in 8.0
EXECUTE, Keyword
EXISTS, Reserved
EXIT, Reserved
EXPANSION, Keyword
EXPIRE, Keyword, added in 5.6.6
EXPLAIN, Reserved
EXPORT, Keyword, added in 5.6.6
EXTENDED, Keyword
EXTENT_SIZE, Keyword
FALSE, Reserved
FAST, Keyword
FAULTS, Keyword
FETCH, Reserved
FIELDS, Keyword
FILE, Keyword
FILE_BLOCK_SIZE, Keyword, added in 5.7
FILTER, Keyword, added in 5.7
FIRST, Keyword
FIRST_VALUE, Reserved, added in 8.0
FIXED, Keyword

FLOAT, Reserved
FLOAT4, Reserved
FLOAT8, Reserved
FLUSH, Keyword
FOLLOWING, Keyword, added in 8.0
FOLLOWS, Keyword, added in 5.7
FOR, Reserved
FORCE, Reserved
FOREIGN, Reserved
FORMAT, Keyword, added in 5.6.5
FOUND, Keyword
FRAC_SECOND, Keyword, removed in 5.5.3
FROM, Reserved
FULL, Keyword
FULLTEXT, Reserved
FUNCTION, Keyword
GENERAL, Keyword, added in 5.5.3; became nonreserved in 5.5.8
GENERATED, Reserved, added in 5.7
GEOMCOLLECTION, Keyword
GEOMETRY, Keyword
GEOMETRYCOLLECTION, Keyword
GET, Reserved, added in 5.6.4
GET_FORMAT, Keyword
GET_MASTER_PUBLIC_KEY, Keyword, added in 8.0
GLOBAL, Keyword
GRANT, Reserved
GRANTS, Keyword
GROUP, Reserved
GROUPING, Reserved, added in 8.0
GROUPS, Reserved, added in 8.0
GROUP_REPLICATION, Keyword, added in 5.7
HANDLER, Keyword
HASH, Keyword
HAVING, Reserved
HELP, Keyword
HIGH_PRIORITY, Reserved
HISTOGRAM, Keyword, added in 8.0
HISTORY, Keyword, added in 8.0
HOST, Keyword
HOSTS, Keyword
HOUR, Keyword
HOUR_MICROSECOND, Reserved
HOUR_MINUTE, Reserved
HOUR_SECOND, Reserved
IDENTIFIED, Keyword
IF, Reserved
IGNORE, Reserved
IGNORE_SERVER_IDS, Keyword, became nonreserved in 5.5.8

—

IMPORT, Keyword
IN, Reserved
INDEX, Reserved
INDEXES, Keyword
INFILE, Reserved
INITIAL_SIZE, Keyword
INNER, Reserved
INNOBASE, Keyword, removed in 5.5.3
INNODB, Keyword, removed in 5.5.3
INOUT, Reserved
INSENSITIVE, Reserved
INSERT, Reserved
INSERT_METHOD, Keyword
INSTALL, Keyword
INSTANCE, Keyword, added in 5.7
INT, Reserved
INT1, Reserved
INT2, Reserved
INT3, Reserved
INT4, Reserved
INT8, Reserved
INTEGER, Reserved
INTERVAL, Reserved
INTO, Reserved
INVISIBLE, Keyword, added in 8.0
INVOKER, Keyword
IO, Keyword
IO_AFTER_GTIDS, Reserved, added in 5.6.5
IO_BEFORE_GTIDS, Reserved, added in 5.6.5
IO_THREAD, Keyword
IPC, Keyword
IS, Reserved
ISOLATION, Keyword
ISSUER, Keyword
ITERATE, Reserved
JOIN, Reserved
JSON, Keyword, added in 5.7
JSON_TABLE, Reserved, added in 8.0
KEY, Reserved
KEYS, Reserved
KEY_BLOCK_SIZE, Keyword
KILL, Reserved
LAG, Reserved, added in 8.0
LANGUAGE, Keyword
LAST, Keyword
LAST_VALUE, Reserved, added in 8.0
LEAD, Reserved, added in 8.0
LEADING, Reserved

LEAVE, Reserved
LEAVES, Keyword
LEFT, Reserved
LESS, Keyword
LEVEL, Keyword
LIKE, Reserved
LIMIT, Reserved
LINEAR, Reserved
LINES, Reserved
LINESTRING, Keyword
LIST, Keyword
LOAD, Reserved
LOCAL, Keyword
LOCALTIME, Reserved
LOCALTIMESTAMP, Reserved
LOCK, Reserved
LOCKED, Keyword, added in 8.0
LOCKS, Keyword
LOGFILE, Keyword
LOGS, Keyword
LONG, Reserved
LONGBLOB, Reserved
LONGTEXT, Reserved
LOOP, Reserved
LOW_PRIORITY, Reserved
MASTER, Keyword
MASTER_AUTO_POSITION, Keyword, added in 5.6.5
MASTER_BIND, Reserved, added in 5.6.1
MASTER_CONNECT_RETRY, Keyword
MASTER_DELAY, Keyword
MASTER_HEARTBEAT_PERIOD, Keyword, became nonreserved in 5.5.8
MASTER_HOST, Keyword
MASTER_LOG_FILE, Keyword
MASTER_LOG_POS, Keyword
MASTER_PASSWORD, Keyword
MASTER_PORT, Keyword
MASTER_PUBLIC_KEY_PATH, Keyword, added in 8.0
MASTER_RETRY_COUNT, Keyword, added in 5.6.1
MASTER_SERVER_ID, Keyword
MASTER_SSL, Keyword
MASTER_SSL_CA, Keyword
MASTER_SSL_CAPATH, Keyword
MASTER_SSL_CERT, Keyword
MASTER_SSL_CIPHER, Keyword
MASTER_SSL_CRL, Keyword, added in 5.6.3
MASTER_SSL_CRLPATH, Keyword, added in 5.6.3
MASTER_SSL_KEY, Keyword
MASTER_SSL_VERIFY_SERVER_CERT, Reserved

MASTER_TLS_VERSION, Keyword, added in 5.7
MASTER_USER, Keyword
MATCH, Reserved
MAXVALUE, Reserved
MAX_CONNECTIONS_PER_HOUR, Keyword
MAX_QUERIES_PER_HOUR, Keyword
MAX_ROWS, Keyword
MAX_SIZE, Keyword
MAX_UPDATES_PER_HOUR, Keyword
MAX_USER_CONNECTIONS, Keyword
MEDIUM, Keyword
MEDIUMBLOB, Reserved
MEDIUMINT, Reserved
MEDIUMTEXT, Reserved
MEMORY, Keyword
MERGE, Keyword
MESSAGE_TEXT, Keyword
MICROSECOND, Keyword
MIDDLEINT, Reserved
MIGRATE, Keyword
MINUTE, Keyword
MINUTE_MICROSECOND, Reserved
MINUTE_SECOND, Reserved
MIN_ROWS, Keyword
MOD, Reserved
MODE, Keyword
MODIFIES, Reserved
MODIFY, Keyword
MONTH, Keyword
MULTILINESTRING, Keyword
MULTIPOINT, Keyword
MULTIPOLYGON, Keyword
MUTEX, Keyword
MYSQL_ERRNO, Keyword
NAME, Keyword
NAMES, Keyword
NATIONAL, Keyword
NATURAL, Reserved
NCHAR, Keyword
NDB, Keyword
NDBCLUSTER, Keyword
NESTED, Keyword, added in 8.0
NEVER, Keyword, added in 5.7
NEW, Keyword
NEXT, Keyword
NO, Keyword
NODEGROUP, Keyword
NONE, Keyword

NOT, Reserved
NOWAIT, Keyword, added in 8.0
NO_WAIT, Keyword
NO_WRITE_TO_BINLOG, Reserved
NTH_VALUE, Reserved, added in 8.0
NTILE, Reserved, added in 8.0
NULL, Reserved
NULLS, Keyword, added in 8.0
NUMBER, Keyword, added in 5.6.4
NUMERIC, Reserved
NVARCHAR, Keyword
OF, Reserved, added in 8.0
OFFSET, Keyword
OLD_PASSWORD, Keyword, removed in 5.7
ON, Reserved
ONE, Keyword
ONE_SHOT, Keyword, became reserved in 5.6.1; removed in 5.6.5
ONLY, Keyword, added in 5.6.5
OPEN, Keyword
OPTIMIZE, Reserved
OPTIMIZER_COSTS, Reserved, added in 5.7
OPTION, Reserved
OPTIONALLY, Reserved
OPTIONS, Keyword
OR, Reserved
ORDER, Reserved
ORDINALITY, Keyword, added in 8.0
OTHERS, Keyword, added in 8.0
OUT, Reserved
OUTER, Reserved
OUTFILE, Reserved
OVER, Reserved, added in 8.0
OWNER, Keyword
PACK_KEYS, Keyword
PAGE, Keyword
PARSER, Keyword
PARSE_GCOL_EXPR, Keyword, added in 5.7; removed in 8.0
PARTIAL, Keyword
PARTITION, Reserved, became reserved in 5.6.2
PARTITIONING, Keyword
PARTITIONS, Keyword
PASSWORD, Keyword
PATH, Keyword, added in 8.0
PERCENT_RANK, Reserved, added in 8.0
PERSIST, Reserved, added in 8.0
PERSIST_ONLY, Reserved, added in 8.0
PHASE, Keyword
PLUGIN, Keyword

—

PLUGINS, Keyword
PLUGIN_DIR, Keyword, added in 5.6.4
POINT, Keyword
POLYGON, Keyword
PORT, Keyword
PRECEDES, Keyword, added in 5.7
PRECEDING, Keyword, added in 8.0
PRECISION, Reserved
PREPARE, Keyword
PRESERVE, Keyword
PREV, Keyword
PRIMARY, Reserved
PRIVILEGES, Keyword
PROCEDURE, Reserved
PROCESS, Keyword, added in 8.0
PROCESSLIST, Keyword
PROFILE, Keyword
PROFILES, Keyword
PROXY, Keyword, added in 5.5.7
PURGE, Reserved
QUARTER, Keyword
QUERY, Keyword
QUICK, Keyword
RANGE, Reserved
RANK, Reserved, added in 8.0
READ, Reserved
READS, Reserved
READ_ONLY, Keyword
READ_WRITE, Reserved
REAL, Reserved
REBUILD, Keyword
RECOVER, Keyword
RECURSIVE, Reserved, added in 8.0
REDOFILE, Keyword, removed in 8.0
REDO_BUFFER_SIZE, Keyword
REDUNDANT, Keyword
REFERENCE, Keyword, added in 8.0
REFERENCES, Reserved
REGEXP, Reserved
RELAY, Keyword, added in 5.5.3
RELAYLOG, Keyword
RELAY_LOG_FILE, Keyword
RELAY_LOG_POS, Keyword
RELAY_THREAD, Keyword
RELEASE, Reserved
RELOAD, Keyword
REMOTE, Keyword, added in 8.0
REMOVE, Keyword

RENAME, Reserved
REORGANIZE, Keyword
REPAIR, Keyword
REPEAT, Reserved
REPEATABLE, Keyword
REPLACE, Reserved
REPLICATE_DO_DB, Keyword, added in 5.7
REPLICATE_DO_TABLE, Keyword, added in 5.7
REPLICATE_IGNORE_DB, Keyword, added in 5.7
REPLICATE_IGNORE_TABLE, Keyword, added in 5.7
REPLICATE_REWRITE_DB, Keyword, added in 5.7
REPLICATE_WILD_DO_TABLE, Keyword, added in 5.7
REPLICATE_WILD_IGNORE_TABLE, Keyword, added in 5.7
REPLICATION, Keyword
REQUIRE, Reserved
RESET, Keyword
RESIGNAL, Reserved
RESOURCE, Keyword, added in 8.0
RESPECT, Keyword, added in 8.0
RESTART, Keyword, added in 8.0
RESTORE, Keyword
RESTRICT, Reserved
RESUME, Keyword
RETURN, Reserved
RETURNED_SQLSTATE, Keyword, added in 5.6.4
RETURNS, Keyword
REUSE, Keyword, added in 8.0
REVERSE, Keyword
REVOKE, Reserved
RIGHT, Reserved
RLIKE, Reserved
ROLE, Keyword, added in 8.0
ROLLBACK, Keyword
ROLLUP, Keyword
ROTATE, Keyword, added in 5.7
ROUTINE, Keyword
ROW, Keyword
ROWS, Keyword
ROW_COUNT, Keyword, added in 5.6.4
ROW_FORMAT, Keyword
ROW_NUMBER, Reserved, added in 8.0
RTREE, Keyword
SAVEPOINT, Keyword
SCHEDULE, Keyword
SCHEMA, Reserved
SCHEMAS, Reserved
SCHEMA_NAME, Keyword
SECOND, Keyword

SECOND_MICROSECOND, Reserved
SECURITY, Keyword
SELECT, Reserved
SENSITIVE, Reserved
SEPARATOR, Reserved
SERIAL, Keyword
SERIALIZABLE, Keyword
SERVER, Keyword
SESSION, Keyword
SET, Reserved
SHARE, Keyword
SHOW, Reserved
SHUTDOWN, Keyword
SIGNAL, Reserved
SIGNED, Keyword
SIMPLE, Keyword
SKIP, Keyword, added in 8.0
SLAVE, Keyword
SLOW, Keyword, added in 5.5.3; became nonreserved in 5.5.8
SMALLINT, Reserved
SNAPSHOT, Keyword
SOCKET, Keyword
SOME, Keyword
SONAME, Keyword
SOUNDS, Keyword
SOURCE, Keyword
SPATIAL, Reserved
SPECIFIC, Reserved
SQL, Reserved
SQLEXCEPTION, Reserved
SQLSTATE, Reserved
SQLWARNING, Reserved
SQL_AFTER_GTIDS, Keyword, added in 5.6.5; became nonreserved in 5.6.6
SQL_AFTER_MTS_GAPS, Keyword, added in 5.6.6
SQL_BEFORE_GTIDS, Keyword, added in 5.6.5; became nonreserved in 5.6.6
SQL_BIG_RESULT, Reserved
SQL_BUFFER_RESULT, Keyword
SQL_CACHE, Keyword, removed in 8.0
SQL_CALC_FOUND_ROWS, Reserved
SQL_NO_CACHE, Keyword
SQL_SMALL_RESULT, Reserved
SQL_THREAD, Keyword
SQL_TSI_DAY, Keyword
SQL_TSI_FRAC_SECOND, Keyword, removed in 5.5.3
SQL_TSI_HOUR, Keyword
SQL_TSI_MINUTE, Keyword
SQL_TSI_MONTH, Keyword
SQL_TSI_QUARTER, Keyword

SQL_TSI_SECOND, Keyword
SQL_TSI_WEEK, Keyword
SQL_TSI_YEAR, Keyword
SRID, Keyword, added in 8.0
SSL, Reserved
STACKED, Keyword, added in 5.7
START, Keyword
STARTING, Reserved
STARTS, Keyword
STATS_AUTO_RECALC, Keyword, added in 5.6.6
STATS_PERSISTENT, Keyword, added in 5.6.6
STATS_SAMPLE_PAGES, Keyword, added in 5.6.6
STATUS, Keyword
STOP, Keyword
STORAGE, Keyword
STORED, Reserved, added in 5.7
STRAIGHT_JOIN, Reserved
STRING, Keyword
SUBCLASS_ORIGIN, Keyword
SUBJECT, Keyword
SUBPARTITION, Keyword
SUBPARTITIONS, Keyword
SUPER, Keyword
SUSPEND, Keyword
SWAPS, Keyword
SWITCHES, Keyword
SYSTEM, Reserved, added in 8.0
TABLE, Reserved
TABLES, Keyword
TABLESPACE, Keyword
TABLE_CHECKSUM, Keyword
TABLE_NAME, Keyword
TEMPORARY, Keyword
TEMPTABLE, Keyword
TERMINATED, Reserved
TEXT, Keyword
THAN, Keyword
THEN, Reserved
THREAD_PRIORITY, Keyword, added in 8.0
TIES, Keyword, added in 8.0
TIME, Keyword
TIMESTAMP, Keyword
TIMESTAMPADD, Keyword
TIMESTAMPDIFF, Keyword
TINYBLOB, Reserved
TINYINT, Reserved
TINYTEXT, Reserved
TO, Reserved

—

TRAILING, Reserved
TRANSACTION, Keyword
TRIGGER, Reserved
TRIGGERS, Keyword
TRUE, Reserved
TRUNCATE, Keyword
TYPE, Keyword
TYPES, Keyword
UNBOUNDED, Keyword, added in 8.0
UNCOMMITTED, Keyword
UNDEFINED, Keyword
UNDO, Reserved
UNDOFILE, Keyword
UNDO_BUFFER_SIZE, Keyword
UNICODE, Keyword
UNINSTALL, Keyword
UNION, Reserved
UNIQUE, Reserved
UNKNOWN, Keyword
UNLOCK, Reserved
UNSIGNED, Reserved
UNTIL, Keyword
UPDATE, Reserved
UPGRADE, Keyword
USAGE, Reserved
USE, Reserved
USER, Keyword
USER_RESOURCES, Keyword
USE_FRM, Keyword
USING, Reserved
UTC_DATE, Reserved
UTC_TIME, Reserved
VALIDATION, Keyword, added in 5.7
VALUES, Reserved
VARBINARY, Reserved
VARCHAR, Reserved
VARCHARACTER, Reserved
VARIABLES, Keyword
VARYING, Reserved
VCPU, Keyword, added in 8.0
VIEW, Keyword
VIRTUAL, Reserved, added in 5.7
VISIBLE, Keyword, added in 8.0
WAIT, Keyword
WARNINGS, Keyword
WEEK, Keyword
WEIGHT_STRING, Keyword
WHEN, Reserved

WHERE, Reserved
WHILE, Reserved
WINDOW, Reserved, added in 8.0
WITH, Reserved
WITHOUT, Keyword, added in 5.7
WORK, Keyword
WRAPPER, Keyword
WRITE, Reserved
X509, Keyword
XA, Keyword
XID, Keyword, added in 5.7
XML, Keyword
XOR, Reserved
YEAR, Keyword
YEAR_MONTH, Reserved
ZEROFILL, Reserved, NULL);

List of Keywords PHP

This list of words have special meaning in PHP.: Even though they may look like functions etc. they are language constructs. You cannot use any of these words as constants, class names, function or method names. Using them as variable names is allowable in most cases, but a real bad idea and could lead to confusion.

As of PHP 7.0.0 these keywords are allowed as property, constant, and method names of classes, interfaces and traits, except that CLASS may not be used as constant name.

PHP Keywords
__ halt_compiler() __ abstract __ and __ array() __ as
break __ callable (as of PHP 5.4) __ case __ catch __ class
clone __ const __ continue __ declare __ default
die() __ do __ echo __ else __ elseif
empty() __ enddeclare __ endfor __ endforeach __ endif
endswitch __ endwhile __ eval() __ exit() __ extends
final __ finally (as of PHP 5.5) __ for __ foreach __ function
global __ goto (as of PHP 5.3) __ if __ implements __
include
include_once __ instanceof __ insteadof (as of PHP 5.4) __
interface __ isset()
list() __ namespace (as of PHP 5.3) __ new __ or __ print
private __ protected __ public __ require __ require_once
return __ static __ switch __ throw __ trait (as of PHP 5.4)
try __ unset() __ use __ var __ while
xor __ yield (as of PHP 5.5) __ __ __
Compile-time constants
__ CLASS __ __ __ DIR __ (as of PHP 5.3) __ __ FILE __
__ __ FUNCTION __ __ __ LINE __ __ __ METHOD __
__ NAMESPACE __ (as of PHP 5.3) __ __ TRAIT __ (as of
PHP 5.4) __ __ __ __

String Functions List

Function __ Description

addcslashes() __ Returns a string with backslashes in front of the specified characters

addslashes() __ Returns a string with backslashes in front of predefined characters

bin2hex() __ Converts a string of ASCII characters to hexadecimal values

chop() __ Removes whitespace or other characters from the right end of a string

chr() __ Returns a character from a specified ASCII value

chunk_split() __ Splits a string into a series of smaller parts

convert_cyr_string() __ Converts a string from one Cyrillic character-set to another

convert_uudecode() __ Decodes a uuencoded string

convert_uuencode() __ Encodes a string using the uuencode algorithm

count_chars() __ Returns information about characters used in a string

crc32() __ Calculates a 32-bit CRC for a string

crypt() __ One-way string hashing

echo() __ Outputs one or more strings

explode() __ Breaks a string into an array

fprintf() __ Writes a formatted string to a specified output stream

get_html_translation_table() __ Returns the translation table used by htmlspecialchars() and htmlentities()

hebrev() __ Converts Hebrew text to visual text

hebrevc() __ Converts Hebrew text to visual text and new lines (\n) into

hex2bin() __ Converts a string of hexadecimal values to ASCII characters html_entity_decode() — Converts HTML entities to characters

htmlentities() — Converts characters to HTML entities

htmlspecialchars_decode() — Converts some predefined HTML entities to characters

htmlspecialchars() — Converts some predefined characters to HTML entities

implode() — Returns a string from the elements of an array

join() — Alias of implode()

lcfirst() — Converts the first character of a string to lowercase

levenshtein() — Returns the Levenshtein distance between two strings

localeconv() — Returns locale numeric and monetary formatting information

ltrim() — Removes whitespace or other characters from the left side of a string

md5() — Calculates the MD5 hash of a string

md5_file() — Calculates the MD5 hash of a file

metaphone() — Calculates the metaphone key of a string

money_format() — Returns a string formatted as a currency string

nl_langinfo() — Returns specific local information

nl2br() — Inserts HTML line breaks in front of each newline in a string

number_format() — Formats a number with grouped thousands

ord() — Returns the ASCII value of the first character of a string

parse_str() — Parses a query string into variables

print() — Outputs one or more strings

printf() — Outputs a formatted string

quoted_printable_decode() — Converts a quoted-printable string to an 8-bit string

quoted_printable_encode() — Converts an 8-bit string to a quoted printable string

—

quotemeta() __ Quotes meta characters

rtrim() __ Removes whitespace or other characters from the right side of a string

setlocale() __ Sets locale information

sha1() __ Calculates the SHA-1 hash of a string

sha1_file() __ Calculates the SHA-1 hash of a file

similar_text() __ Calculates the similarity between two strings

soundex() __ Calculates the soundex key of a string

sprintf() __ Writes a formatted string to a variable

sscanf() __ Parses input from a string according to a format

str_getcsv() __ Parses a CSV string into an array

str_ireplace() __ Replaces some characters in a string (case-insensitive)

str_pad() __ Pads a string to a new length

str_repeat() __ Repeats a string a specified number of times

str_replace () __ Replaces some characters in a string (case-sensitive)

str_rot13() __ Performs the ROT13 encoding on a string

str_shuffle() __ Randomly shuffles all characters in a string

str_split() __ Splits a string into an array

str_word_count() __ Count the number of words in a string

strcasecmp() __ Compares two strings (case-insensitive)

strchr() __ Finds the first occurrence of a string inside another string (alias of strstr())

strcmp() __ Compares two strings (case-sensitive)

strcoll() __ Compares two strings (locale based string comparison)

strcspn() __ Returns the number of characters found in a string before any part of some specified characters are found

strip_tags() __ Strips HTML and PHP tags from a string

stripcslashes() __ Unquotes a string quoted with addcslashes()

stripslashes() __ Unquotes a string quoted with addslashes()

stripos() __ Returns the position of the first occurrence of a string inside another string (case-insensitive) stristr() — Finds the first occurrence of a string inside another string (case-insensitive)

strlen() — Returns the length of a string

strnatcasecmp() — Compares two strings using a "natural order" algorithm (case-insensitive)

strnatcmp() — Compares two strings using a "natural order" algorithm (case-sensitive)

strncasecmp() — String comparison of the first n characters (case-insensitive)

strncmp() — String comparison of the first n characters (case-sensitive)

strpbrk() — Searches a string for any of a set of characters

strpos() — Returns the position of the first occurrence of a string inside another string (case-sensitive)

strrchr() — Finds the last occurrence of a string inside another string

strrev() — Reverses a string

strripos() — Finds the position of the last occurrence of a string inside another string (case-insensitive)

strrpos() — Finds the position of the last occurrence of a string inside another string (case-sensitive)

strspn() — Returns the number of characters found in a string that contains only characters from a specified charlist

strstr() — Finds the first occurrence of a string inside another string (case-sensitive)

strtok() — Splits a string into smaller strings

strtolower() — Converts a string to lowercase letters

strtoupper() — Converts a string to uppercase letters

strtr() — Translates certain characters in a string

substr () — Returns a part of a string

substr_compare() — Compares two strings from a specified start position (binary safe and optionally case-sensitive)

substr_count() — Counts the number of times a substring occurs in a string

substr_replace () — Replaces a part of a string with another string

—

trim() __ Removes whitespace or other characters from both sides of a string

ucfirst() __ Converts the first character of a string to uppercase

ucwords() __ Converts the first character of each word in a string to uppercase

vfprintf() __ Writes a formatted string to a specified output stream

vprintf() __ Outputs a formatted string

vsprintf() __ Writes a formatted string to a variable

wordwrap() __ Wraps a string to a given number of characters

Session Commands ¶

session_abort __ Discard session array changes and finish session

session_cache_expire __ Return current cache expire

session_cache_limiter __ Get and/or set the current cache limiter

session_commit __ Alias of session_write_close

session_create_id __ Create new session id (php 7)

session_decode __ Decodes session data from a session encoded string

session_destroy __ Destroys all data registered to a session

session_encode __ Encodes the current session data as a session encoded string

session_gc __ Perform session data garbage collection

session_get_cookie_params __ Get the session cookie parameters

session_id __ Get and/or set the current session id

session_is_registered __ Find out whether a global variable is registered in a session

session_module_name __ Get and/or set the current session module

session_name __ Get and/or set the current session name

session_regenerate_id __ Update the current session id with a newly generated one

session_register_shutdown __ Session shutdown function

session_register __ Register one or more global variables with the current session

session_reset __ Re-initialize session array with original values

session_save_path __ Get and/or set the current session save path

session_set_cookie_params __ Set the session cookie parameters

session_set_save_handler __ Sets user-level session storage functions

session_start __ Start new or resume existing session

session_status __ Returns the current session status

session_unregister __ Unregister a global variable from the current session

session_unset __ Free all session variables

session_write_close __ Write session data and end session

New in php 7

session_start() now accepts an array of options that override the session configuration directives normally set in php.ini.

```
session_start([
'cache_limiter'=>'private',
'read_and_close'=>true,
]);
```

—

Time Zone List

CITY __ UTC/GMT
Africa/Abidjan __ UTC/GMT +00:00
Africa/Accra __ UTC/GMT +00:00
Africa/Addis_Ababa __ UTC/GMT +03:00
Africa/Algiers __ UTC/GMT +01:00
Africa/Asmara __ UTC/GMT +03:00
Africa/Bamako __ UTC/GMT +00:00
Africa/Bangui __ UTC/GMT +01:00
Africa/Banjul __ UTC/GMT +00:00
Africa/Bissau __ UTC/GMT +00:00
Africa/Blantyre __ UTC/GMT +02:00
Africa/Brazzaville __ UTC/GMT +01:00
Africa/Bujumbura __ UTC/GMT +02:00
Africa/Cairo __ UTC/GMT +02:00
Africa/Casablanca __ UTC/GMT +01:00
Africa/Ceuta __ UTC/GMT +02:00
Africa/Conakry __ UTC/GMT +00:00
Africa/Dakar __ UTC/GMT +00:00
Africa/Dar_es_Salaam __ UTC/GMT +03:00
Africa/Djibouti __ UTC/GMT +03:00
Africa/Douala __ UTC/GMT +01:00
Africa/El_Aaiun __ UTC/GMT +01:00
Africa/Freetown __ UTC/GMT +00:00
Africa/Gaborone __ UTC/GMT +02:00
Africa/Harare __ UTC/GMT +02:00
Africa/Johannesburg __ UTC/GMT +02:00
Africa/Juba __ UTC/GMT +03:00
Africa/Kampala __ UTC/GMT +03:00
Africa/Khartoum __ UTC/GMT +02:00
Africa/Kigali __ UTC/GMT +02:00
Africa/Kinshasa __ UTC/GMT +01:00
Africa/Lagos __ UTC/GMT +01:00
Africa/Libreville __ UTC/GMT +01:00

Africa/Lome __ UTC/GMT +00:00
Africa/Luanda __ UTC/GMT +01:00
Africa/Lubumbashi __ UTC/GMT +02:00
Africa/Lusaka __ UTC/GMT +02:00
Africa/Malabo __ UTC/GMT +01:00
Africa/Maputo __ UTC/GMT +02:00
Africa/Maseru __ UTC/GMT +02:00
Africa/Mbabane __ UTC/GMT +02:00
Africa/Mogadishu __ UTC/GMT +03:00
Africa/Monrovia __ UTC/GMT +00:00
Africa/Nairobi __ UTC/GMT +03:00
Africa/Ndjamena __ UTC/GMT +01:00
Africa/Niamey __ UTC/GMT +01:00
Africa/Nouakchott __ UTC/GMT +00:00
Africa/Ouagadougou __ UTC/GMT +00:00
Africa/Porto-Novo __ UTC/GMT +01:00
Africa/Sao_Tome __ UTC/GMT +01:00
Africa/Tripoli __ UTC/GMT +02:00
Africa/Tunis __ UTC/GMT +01:00
Africa/Windhoek __ UTC/GMT +02:00
America/Adak __ UTC/GMT -09:00
America/Anchorage __ UTC/GMT -08:00
America/Anguilla __ UTC/GMT -04:00
America/Antigua __ UTC/GMT -04:00
America/Araguaina __ UTC/GMT -03:00
America/Argentina/Buenos_Aires __ UTC/GMT -03:00
America/Argentina/Catamarca __ UTC/GMT -03:00
America/Argentina/Cordoba __ UTC/GMT -03:00
America/Argentina/Jujuy __ UTC/GMT -03:00
America/Argentina/La_Rioja __ UTC/GMT -03:00
America/Argentina/Mendoza __ UTC/GMT -03:00
America/Argentina/Rio_Gallegos __ UTC/GMT -03:00
America/Argentina/Salta __ UTC/GMT -03:00
America/Argentina/San_Juan __ UTC/GMT -03:00
America/Argentina/San_Luis __ UTC/GMT -03:00
America/Argentina/Tucuman __ UTC/GMT -03:00

—

America/Argentina/Ushuaia __ UTC/GMT -03:00
America/Aruba __ UTC/GMT -04:00
America/Asuncion __ UTC/GMT -04:00
America/Atikokan __ UTC/GMT -05:00
America/Bahia __ UTC/GMT -03:00
America/Bahia_Banderas __ UTC/GMT -05:00
America/Barbados __ UTC/GMT -04:00
America/Belem __ UTC/GMT -03:00
America/Belize __ UTC/GMT -06:00
America/Blanc-Sablon __ UTC/GMT -04:00
America/Boa_Vista __ UTC/GMT -04:00
America/Bogota __ UTC/GMT -05:00
America/Boise __ UTC/GMT -06:00
America/Cambridge_Bay __ UTC/GMT -06:00
America/Campo_Grande __ UTC/GMT -04:00
America/Cancun __ UTC/GMT -05:00
America/Caracas __ UTC/GMT -04:00
America/Cayenne __ UTC/GMT -03:00
America/Cayman __ UTC/GMT -05:00
America/Chicago __ UTC/GMT -05:00
America/Chihuahua __ UTC/GMT -06:00
America/Costa_Rica __ UTC/GMT -06:00
America/Creston __ UTC/GMT -07:00
America/Cuiaba __ UTC/GMT -04:00
America/Curacao __ UTC/GMT -04:00
America/Danmarkshavn __ UTC/GMT +00:00
America/Dawson __ UTC/GMT -07:00
America/Dawson_Creek __ UTC/GMT -07:00
America/Denver __ UTC/GMT -06:00
America/Detroit __ UTC/GMT -04:00
America/Dominica __ UTC/GMT -04:00
America/Edmonton __ UTC/GMT -06:00
America/Eirunepe __ UTC/GMT -05:00
America/El_Salvador __ UTC/GMT -06:00
America/Fort_Nelson __ UTC/GMT -07:00
America/Fortaleza __ UTC/GMT -03:00

America/Glace_Bay __ UTC/GMT -03:00
America/Godthab __ UTC/GMT -02:00
America/Goose_Bay __ UTC/GMT -03:00
America/Grand_Turk __ UTC/GMT -04:00
America/Grenada __ UTC/GMT -04:00
America/Guadeloupe __ UTC/GMT -04:00
America/Guatemala __ UTC/GMT -06:00
America/Guayaquil __ UTC/GMT -05:00
America/Guyana __ UTC/GMT -04:00
America/Halifax __ UTC/GMT -03:00
America/Havana __ UTC/GMT -04:00
America/Hermosillo __ UTC/GMT -07:00
America/Indiana/Indianapolis __ UTC/GMT -04:00
America/Indiana/Knox __ UTC/GMT -05:00
America/Indiana/Marengo __ UTC/GMT -04:00
America/Indiana/Petersburg __ UTC/GMT -04:00
America/Indiana/Tell_City __ UTC/GMT -05:00
America/Indiana/Vevay __ UTC/GMT -04:00
America/Indiana/Vincennes __ UTC/GMT -04:00
America/Indiana/Winamac __ UTC/GMT -04:00
America/Inuvik __ UTC/GMT -06:00
America/Iqaluit __ UTC/GMT -04:00
America/Jamaica __ UTC/GMT -05:00
America/Juneau __ UTC/GMT -08:00
America/Kentucky/Louisville __ UTC/GMT -04:00
America/Kentucky/Monticello __ UTC/GMT -04:00
America/Kralendijk __ UTC/GMT -04:00
America/La_Paz __ UTC/GMT -04:00
America/Lima __ UTC/GMT -05:00
America/Los_Angeles __ UTC/GMT -07:00
America/Lower_Princes __ UTC/GMT -04:00
America/Maceio __ UTC/GMT -03:00
America/Managua __ UTC/GMT -06:00
America/Manaus __ UTC/GMT -04:00
America/Marigot __ UTC/GMT -04:00
America/Martinique __ UTC/GMT -04:00

—

America/Matamoros __ UTC/GMT -05:00
America/Mazatlan __ UTC/GMT -06:00
America/Menominee __ UTC/GMT -05:00
America/Merida __ UTC/GMT -05:00
America/Metlakatla __ UTC/GMT -08:00
America/Mexico_City __ UTC/GMT -05:00
America/Miquelon __ UTC/GMT -02:00
America/Moncton __ UTC/GMT -03:00
America/Monterrey __ UTC/GMT -05:00
America/Montevideo __ UTC/GMT -03:00
America/Montserrat __ UTC/GMT -04:00
America/Nassau __ UTC/GMT -04:00
America/New_York __ UTC/GMT -04:00
America/Nipigon __ UTC/GMT -04:00
America/Nome __ UTC/GMT -08:00
America/Noronha __ UTC/GMT -02:00
America/North_Dakota/Beulah __ UTC/GMT -05:00
America/North_Dakota/Center __ UTC/GMT -05:00
America/North_Dakota/New_Salem __ UTC/GMT -05:00
America/Ojinaga __ UTC/GMT -06:00
America/Panama __ UTC/GMT -05:00
America/Pangnirtung __ UTC/GMT -04:00
America/Paramaribo __ UTC/GMT -03:00
America/Phoenix __ UTC/GMT -07:00
America/Port-au-Prince __ UTC/GMT -04:00
America/Port_of_Spain __ UTC/GMT -04:00
America/Porto_Velho __ UTC/GMT -04:00
America/Puerto_Rico __ UTC/GMT -04:00
America/Punta_Arenas __ UTC/GMT -03:00
America/Rainy_River __ UTC/GMT -05:00
America/Rankin_Inlet __ UTC/GMT -05:00
America/Recife __ UTC/GMT -03:00
America/Regina __ UTC/GMT -06:00
America/Resolute __ UTC/GMT -05:00
America/Rio_Branco __ UTC/GMT -05:00
America/Santarem __ UTC/GMT -03:00

America/Santiago __ UTC/GMT -03:00
America/Santo_Domingo __ UTC/GMT -04:00
America/Sao_Paulo __ UTC/GMT -03:00
America/Scoresbysund __ UTC/GMT +00:00
America/Sitka __ UTC/GMT -08:00
America/St_Barthelemy __ UTC/GMT -04:00
America/St_Johns __ UTC/GMT -02:30
America/St_Kitts __ UTC/GMT -04:00
America/St_Lucia __ UTC/GMT -04:00
America/St_Thomas __ UTC/GMT -04:00
America/St_Vincent __ UTC/GMT -04:00
America/Swift_Current __ UTC/GMT -06:00
America/Tegucigalpa __ UTC/GMT -06:00
America/Thule __ UTC/GMT -03:00
America/Thunder_Bay __ UTC/GMT -04:00
America/Tijuana __ UTC/GMT -07:00
America/Toronto __ UTC/GMT -04:00
America/Tortola __ UTC/GMT -04:00
America/Vancouver __ UTC/GMT -07:00
America/Whitehorse __ UTC/GMT -07:00
America/Winnipeg __ UTC/GMT -05:00
America/Yakutat __ UTC/GMT -08:00
America/Yellowknife __ UTC/GMT -06:00
Antarctica/Casey __ UTC/GMT +11:00
Antarctica/Davis __ UTC/GMT +07:00
Antarctica/DumontDUrville __ UTC/GMT +10:00
Antarctica/Macquarie __ UTC/GMT +11:00
Antarctica/Mawson __ UTC/GMT +05:00
Antarctica/McMurdo __ UTC/GMT +12:00
Antarctica/Palmer __ UTC/GMT -03:00
Antarctica/Rothera __ UTC/GMT -03:00
Antarctica/Syowa __ UTC/GMT +03:00
Antarctica/Troll __ UTC/GMT +02:00
Antarctica/Vostok __ UTC/GMT +06:00
Arctic/Longyearbyen __ UTC/GMT +02:00
Asia/Aden __ UTC/GMT +03:00

—

Asia/Almaty __ UTC/GMT +06:00
Asia/Amman __ UTC/GMT +03:00
Asia/Anadyr __ UTC/GMT +12:00
Asia/Aqtau __ UTC/GMT +05:00
Asia/Aqtobe __ UTC/GMT +05:00
Asia/Ashgabat __ UTC/GMT +05:00
Asia/Atyrau __ UTC/GMT +05:00
Asia/Baghdad __ UTC/GMT +03:00
Asia/Bahrain __ UTC/GMT +03:00
Asia/Baku __ UTC/GMT +04:00
Asia/Bangkok __ UTC/GMT +07:00
Asia/Barnaul __ UTC/GMT +07:00
Asia/Beirut __ UTC/GMT +03:00
Asia/Bishkek __ UTC/GMT +06:00
Asia/Brunei __ UTC/GMT +08:00
Asia/Chita __ UTC/GMT +09:00
Asia/Choibalsan __ UTC/GMT +08:00
Asia/Colombo __ UTC/GMT +05:30
Asia/Damascus __ UTC/GMT +03:00
Asia/Dhaka __ UTC/GMT +06:00
Asia/Dili __ UTC/GMT +09:00
Asia/Dubai __ UTC/GMT +04:00
Asia/Dushanbe __ UTC/GMT +05:00
Asia/Famagusta __ UTC/GMT +03:00
Asia/Gaza __ UTC/GMT +03:00
Asia/Hebron __ UTC/GMT +03:00
Asia/Ho_Chi_Minh __ UTC/GMT +07:00
Asia/Hong_Kong __ UTC/GMT +08:00
Asia/Hovd __ UTC/GMT +07:00
Asia/Irkutsk __ UTC/GMT +08:00
Asia/Jakarta __ UTC/GMT +07:00
Asia/Jayapura __ UTC/GMT +09:00
Asia/Jerusalem __ UTC/GMT +03:00
Asia/Kabul __ UTC/GMT +04:30
Asia/Kamchatka __ UTC/GMT +12:00
Asia/Karachi __ UTC/GMT +05:00

Asia/Kathmandu __ UTC/GMT +05:45

Asia/Khandyga __ UTC/GMT +09:00

Asia/Kolkata __ UTC/GMT +05:30

Asia/Krasnoyarsk __ UTC/GMT +07:00

Asia/Kuala_Lumpur __ UTC/GMT +08:00

Asia/Kuching __ UTC/GMT +08:00

Asia/Kuwait __ UTC/GMT +03:00

Asia/Macau __ UTC/GMT +08:00

Asia/Magadan __ UTC/GMT +11:00

Asia/Makassar __ UTC/GMT +08:00

Asia/Manila __ UTC/GMT +08:00

Asia/Muscat __ UTC/GMT +04:00

Asia/Nicosia __ UTC/GMT +03:00

Asia/Novokuznetsk __ UTC/GMT +07:00

Asia/Novosibirsk __ UTC/GMT +07:00

Asia/Omsk __ UTC/GMT +06:00

Asia/Oral __ UTC/GMT +05:00

Asia/Phnom_Penh __ UTC/GMT +07:00

Asia/Pontianak __ UTC/GMT +07:00

Asia/Pyongyang __ UTC/GMT +08:30

Asia/Qatar __ UTC/GMT +03:00

Asia/Qyzylorda __ UTC/GMT +06:00

Asia/Riyadh __ UTC/GMT +03:00

Asia/Sakhalin __ UTC/GMT +11:00

Asia/Samarkand __ UTC/GMT +05:00

Asia/Seoul __ UTC/GMT +09:00

Asia/Shanghai __ UTC/GMT +08:00

Asia/Singapore __ UTC/GMT +08:00

Asia/Srednekolymsk __ UTC/GMT +11:00

Asia/Taipei __ UTC/GMT +08:00

Asia/Tashkent __ UTC/GMT +05:00

Asia/Tbilisi __ UTC/GMT +04:00

Asia/Tehran __ UTC/GMT +04:30

Asia/Thimphu __ UTC/GMT +06:00

Asia/Tokyo __ UTC/GMT +09:00

Asia/Tomsk __ UTC/GMT +07:00

—

Asia/Ulaanbaatar __ UTC/GMT +08:00
Asia/Urumqi __ UTC/GMT +06:00
Asia/Ust-Nera __ UTC/GMT +10:00
Asia/Vientiane __ UTC/GMT +07:00
Asia/Vladivostok __ UTC/GMT +10:00
Asia/Yakutsk __ UTC/GMT +09:00
Asia/Yangon __ UTC/GMT +06:30
Asia/Yekaterinburg __ UTC/GMT +05:00
Asia/Yerevan __ UTC/GMT +04:00
Atlantic/Azores __ UTC/GMT +00:00
Atlantic/Bermuda __ UTC/GMT -03:00
Atlantic/Canary __ UTC/GMT +01:00
Atlantic/Cape_Verde __ UTC/GMT -01:00
Atlantic/Faroe __ UTC/GMT +01:00
Atlantic/Madeira __ UTC/GMT +01:00
Atlantic/Reykjavik __ UTC/GMT +00:00
Atlantic/South_Georgia __ UTC/GMT -02:00
Atlantic/St_Helena __ UTC/GMT +00:00
Atlantic/Stanley __ UTC/GMT -03:00
Australia/Adelaide __ UTC/GMT +09:30
Australia/Brisbane __ UTC/GMT +10:00
Australia/Broken_Hill __ UTC/GMT +09:30
Australia/Currie __ UTC/GMT +10:00
Australia/Darwin __ UTC/GMT +09:30
Australia/Eucla __ UTC/GMT +08:45
Australia/Hobart __ UTC/GMT +10:00
Australia/Lindeman __ UTC/GMT +10:00
Australia/Lord_Howe __ UTC/GMT +10:30
Australia/Melbourne __ UTC/GMT +10:00
Australia/Perth __ UTC/GMT +08:00
Australia/Sydney __ UTC/GMT +10:00
Europe/Amsterdam __ UTC/GMT +02:00
Europe/Andorra __ UTC/GMT +02:00
Europe/Astrakhan __ UTC/GMT +04:00
Europe/Athens __ UTC/GMT +03:00
Europe/Belgrade __ UTC/GMT +02:00

Europe/Berlin __ UTC/GMT +02:00
Europe/Bratislava __ UTC/GMT +02:00
Europe/Brussels __ UTC/GMT +02:00
Europe/Bucharest __ UTC/GMT +03:00
Europe/Budapest __ UTC/GMT +02:00
Europe/Busingen __ UTC/GMT +02:00
Europe/Chisinau __ UTC/GMT +03:00
Europe/Copenhagen __ UTC/GMT +02:00
Europe/Dublin __ UTC/GMT +01:00
Europe/Gibraltar __ UTC/GMT +02:00
Europe/Guernsey __ UTC/GMT +01:00
Europe/Helsinki __ UTC/GMT +03:00
Europe/Isle_of_Man __ UTC/GMT +01:00
Europe/Istanbul __ UTC/GMT +03:00
Europe/Jersey __ UTC/GMT +01:00
Europe/Kaliningrad __ UTC/GMT +02:00
Europe/Kiev __ UTC/GMT +03:00
Europe/Kirov __ UTC/GMT +03:00
Europe/Lisbon __ UTC/GMT +01:00
Europe/Ljubljana __ UTC/GMT +02:00
Europe/London __ UTC/GMT +01:00
Europe/Luxembourg __ UTC/GMT +02:00
Europe/Madrid __ UTC/GMT +02:00
Europe/Malta __ UTC/GMT +02:00
Europe/Mariehamn __ UTC/GMT +03:00
Europe/Minsk __ UTC/GMT +03:00
Europe/Monaco __ UTC/GMT +02:00
Europe/Moscow __ UTC/GMT +03:00
Europe/Oslo __ UTC/GMT +02:00
Europe/Paris __ UTC/GMT +02:00
Europe/Podgorica __ UTC/GMT +02:00
Europe/Prague __ UTC/GMT +02:00
Europe/Riga __ UTC/GMT +03:00
Europe/Rome __ UTC/GMT +02:00
Europe/Samara __ UTC/GMT +04:00
Europe/San_Marino __ UTC/GMT +02:00

__

Europe/Sarajevo __ UTC/GMT +02:00
Europe/Saratov __ UTC/GMT +04:00
Europe/Simferopol __ UTC/GMT +03:00
Europe/Skopje __ UTC/GMT +02:00
Europe/Sofia __ UTC/GMT +03:00
Europe/Stockholm __ UTC/GMT +02:00
Europe/Tallinn __ UTC/GMT +03:00
Europe/Tirane __ UTC/GMT +02:00
Europe/Ulyanovsk __ UTC/GMT +04:00
Europe/Uzhgorod __ UTC/GMT +03:00
Europe/Vaduz __ UTC/GMT +02:00
Europe/Vatican __ UTC/GMT +02:00
Europe/Vienna __ UTC/GMT +02:00
Europe/Vilnius __ UTC/GMT +03:00
Europe/Volgograd __ UTC/GMT +03:00
Europe/Warsaw __ UTC/GMT +02:00
Europe/Zagreb __ UTC/GMT +02:00
Europe/Zaporozhye __ UTC/GMT +03:00
Europe/Zurich __ UTC/GMT +02:00
Indian/Antananarivo __ UTC/GMT +03:00
Indian/Chagos __ UTC/GMT +06:00
Indian/Christmas __ UTC/GMT +07:00
Indian/Cocos __ UTC/GMT +06:30
Indian/Comoro __ UTC/GMT +03:00
Indian/Kerguelen __ UTC/GMT +05:00
Indian/Mahe __ UTC/GMT +04:00
Indian/Maldives __ UTC/GMT +05:00
Indian/Mauritius __ UTC/GMT +04:00
Indian/Mayotte __ UTC/GMT +03:00
Indian/Reunion __ UTC/GMT +04:00
Pacific/Apia __ UTC/GMT +13:00
Pacific/Auckland __ UTC/GMT +12:00
Pacific/Bougainville __ UTC/GMT +11:00
Pacific/Chatham __ UTC/GMT +12:45
Pacific/Chuuk __ UTC/GMT +10:00
Pacific/Easter __ UTC/GMT -05:00

Pacific/Efate __ UTC/GMT +11:00
Pacific/Enderbury __ UTC/GMT +13:00
Pacific/Fakaofo __ UTC/GMT +13:00
Pacific/Fiji __ UTC/GMT +12:00
Pacific/Funafuti __ UTC/GMT +12:00
Pacific/Galapagos __ UTC/GMT -06:00
Pacific/Gambier __ UTC/GMT -09:00
Pacific/Guadalcanal __ UTC/GMT +11:00
Pacific/Guam __ UTC/GMT +10:00
Pacific/Honolulu __ UTC/GMT -10:00
Pacific/Kiritimati __ UTC/GMT +14:00
Pacific/Kosrae __ UTC/GMT +11:00
Pacific/Kwajalein __ UTC/GMT +12:00
Pacific/Majuro __ UTC/GMT +12:00
Pacific/Marquesas __ UTC/GMT -09:30
Pacific/Midway __ UTC/GMT -11:00
Pacific/Nauru __ UTC/GMT +12:00
Pacific/Niue __ UTC/GMT -11:00
Pacific/Norfolk __ UTC/GMT +11:00
Pacific/Noumea __ UTC/GMT +11:00
Pacific/Pago_Pago __ UTC/GMT -11:00
Pacific/Palau __ UTC/GMT +09:00
Pacific/Pitcairn __ UTC/GMT -08:00
Pacific/Pohnpei __ UTC/GMT +11:00
Pacific/Port_Moresby __ UTC/GMT +10:00
Pacific/Rarotonga __ UTC/GMT -10:00
Pacific/Saipan __ UTC/GMT +10:00
Pacific/Tahiti __ UTC/GMT -10:00
Pacific/Tarawa __ UTC/GMT +12:00
Pacific/Tongatapu __ UTC/GMT +13:00
Pacific/Wake __ UTC/GMT +12:00
Pacific/Wallis __ UTC/GMT +12:00
UTC __ UTC/GMT +00:00

—

Date Format Characters List

The following characters are recognized in the `format` parameter string
parameter string
`format` **character**
Description
Example returned values
DAY

D

Day of the month, 2 digits with leading zeros

01 to 31

D

A textual representation of a day, three letters

MON through SUN

J

Day of the month without leading zeros

1 to 31

L (lowercase 'L')

A full textual representation of the day of the week

SUNDAY through SATURDAY

N

ISO-8601 numeric representation of the day of the week (added in PHP 5.1.0)

1 (for Monday) through 7 (for Sunday)

S

English ordinal suffix for the day of the month, 2 characters

ST, ND, RD or TH. Works well with J

W

Numeric representation of the day of the week

0 (for Sunday) through 6 (for Saturday)

Z

The day of the year (starting from 0)

0 through 365

WEEK

W

ISO-8601 week number of year, weeks starting on Monday

Example: 42 (the 42nd week in the year)

MONTH

F

A full textual representation of a month, such as January or March

JANUARY through DECEMBER

M

Numeric representation of a month, with leading zeros

01 through 12

M

A short textual representation of a month, three letters

JAN through DEC

N

Numeric representation of a month, without leading zeros

1 through 12

T

Number of days in the given month

28 through 31

YEAR

L

Whether it's a leap year

1 if it is a leap year, 0 otherwise.

O

ISO-8601 week-numbering year. This has the same value as Y, except that if the ISO week number (W) belongs to the previous or next year, that year is used instead. (added in PHP 5.1.0)

Examples: 1999 or 2003

Y

A full numeric representation of a year, 4 digits

Examples: 1999 or 2003

Y

A two digit representation of a year

—

Examples: 99 or 03

A

Lowercase Ante meridiem and Post meridiem

AM or PM

A

Uppercase Ante meridiem and Post meridiem

AM or PM

B

Swatch Internet time

000 through 999

G

12-hour format of an hour without leading zeros

1 through 12

G

24-hour format of an hour without leading zeros

0 through 23

H

12-hour format of an hour with leading zeros

01 through 12

H

24-hour format of an hour with leading zeros

00 through 23

I

Minutes with leading zeros

00 to 59

S

Seconds, with leading zeros

00 through 59

U

Microseconds (added in PHP 5.2.2). Note that **date()** will always generate 000000 since it takes an integer parameter, whereas DateTime::format() does support microseconds if DateTime was created with microseconds.

Example: 654321

V

Milliseconds (added in PHP 7.0.0). Same note applies as for U.

Example: 654

TIMEZONE

E

Timezone identifier (added in PHP 5.1.0)

Examples: UTC, GMT, ATLANTIC/AZORES

I (capital i)

Whether or not the date is in daylight saving time

1 if Daylight Saving Time, 0 otherwise.

O

Difference to Greenwich time (GMT) in hours

Example: +0200

P

Difference to Greenwich time (GMT) with colon between hours and minutes (added in PHP 5.1.3)

Example: +02:00

T

Timezone abbreviation

Examples: EST, MDT ...

Z

Timezone offset in seconds. The offset for timezones west of UTC is always negative, and for those east of UTC is always positive.

-43200 through 50400

FULL DATE/TIME

C

ISO 8601 date (added in PHP 5)

2004-02-12T15:19:21+00:00

R

» RFC 2822 formatted date

Example: THU, 21 DEC 2000 16:01:07 +0200

U

Seconds since the Unix Epoch (January 1 1970 00:00:00 GMT)

—

See also time()

Other Books by James Blanchette

Interrogate SEO
Interrogate Web Designers
Theo
Theo2
Plato Raw

—

www.ingramcontent.com/pod-product-compliance
Lightning Source LLC
Chambersburg PA
CBHW031239050326
40690CB00007B/864